D1568993

DR. GILDA CARLE

An Imprint of HarperCollins*Publishers*

For my beautiful and brilliant niece-consultant,
Erin Gallins, and for all the other adolescent
and teenage girls who deserve to know more

HarperCollins books may be purchased for educational, business, or sales promotional use. For information please write: Special Markets Department, HarperCollins Publishers Inc., 10 East 53rd Street, New York, NY 10022.

FIRST EDITION

Designed by Nicola Ferguson

Library of Congress Cataloging-in-Publication Data
Carle, Gilda.
He's not all that! : how to attract
the good guys / by Gilda Carle.
p.   cm.
ISBN 0-06-019924-5
1. Mate selection.   2. Man-woman relationships.
I. Title: How to attract the good guys.   II. Title
HQ801 .C2774 2001
646.7'7—dc21   00-043062

97 98 99 00 01 RRD 10 9 8 7 6 5 4 3 2 1

CONTENTS

Acknowledgments *vii*

Introduction *ix*

PART I

WHAT GIRLS *WANT*: 2 Hits to Happiness *1*

Want #1: Loyal Girlfriends *3*

Want #2: A Cool Boyfriend *41*

PART II

WHAT GIRLS *NEED*: 4 Secrets of Love *61*

Need #1: Be an *It Girl* *69*

Need #2: Understand Guys *119*

Need #3: Create Your Own Excitement *207*

Need #4: Make Him a Teammate Before
a Soulmate *255*

CONCLUSION

How to Attract the Good Guys *277*

ACKNOWLEDGMENTS

I am eternally grateful to five women who believed in this project and supported my efforts. Laura Yorke insisted I write this book, Lara Asher helped mold it, Diane Reverend bought it, Janet Dery edited it, and Anke Steineke fine-tuned the contract for it. Thank you all for believing *He's Not All That!* needed to be out there.

Thank you, Mercy College, New York, especially Andy Joppa, Tom Milton, and Wayne Ciofarri, who have appreciated and encouraged my mission to make the world's relationships easier and more productive. Also, kisses to my mom and my niece, Lauren Gallins, for your faith in me.

Special thanks to my friends Elizabeth Hepburn, Liz Gassett, and Martin Arnold and to my sister Kathi, all of whom stood by me during my darker days. Thank you for reminding me that eventually I'd find the light.

And to all my fans who continue to stop me in the street, at malls, at airports, and restaurants, who ask when I'm next going to be on TV, and who graciously offer your kind words of support. May your relationships be richer as a result of this book.

INTRODUCTION

Welcome to the new group of millennium teens called "Generation Y," the first generation in history to grow up with computers. Studies tell us that teenagers spend 4.2 hours a week logging on at home, and another 2.3 hours a week logging on elsewhere. Teen Research Unlimited says that teens spend time on-line doing research, sending and reading e-mail, playing games, and surfing for things to buy. The Kaiser Family Foundation says that kids age 2 to 18 spend 5 hours and 29 minutes, 7 days a week, watching TV, listening to music, or working on a home computer. While many of you also read each day for fun—not just for homework—the majority of your time is spent with TV, computers, and video games. So how does this information affect your life?

For starters, the face-to-face interaction that kids used to enjoy has greatly diminished. Outside of school, many teens find themselves totally alone, pursuing individual activities that don't include others. As a result, although Gen-Y is plugged in and logged on, you are missing out on a lot of the necessary people skills that teach you how to be comfortable and successful in getting along with girlfriends and boyfriends. The e-mail I receive from teens around the world constantly asks me to help solve communication problems. That's why I decided to write this book. But that wasn't the only reason.

After I wrote *Don't Bet on the Prince! How to Have the Man You Want by Betting on Yourself,* I received a lot of mail from adult women. At about the same time, I had listed my new web address on my "Love Doctor" column in *Teen Magazine,* so I was also receiving tons of e-mail from teenage girls like you. With all the incoming correspondence, I discovered an astonishing fact. The issues for adult women and those for teenage girls were the same. Without exception, I realized that all females' problems with the opposite sex center around three issues: how to hook him, hug him, and hold him. The women and girls asked the same questions, from finding Mr. Right to keeping Mr. Right, from friends becoming lovers to lovers becoming friends, from dumping and being dumped to lying, cheating, and love triangles. A sad pattern emerges: the unresolved issues that girls had with their boyfriends naturally grew into the same issues that perplex women in their relationships with men.

The world recently watched the violent massacre at Columbine High School. Researchers found many similar incidents around the nation. As experts search for ways to prevent these horrors from recurring, the obvious finger-pointing put the media, films, video games, TV, and gun availability on the line. Not so obvious was the fact that the perpetrators were all boys. The experts began to ask, "Why?"

Unlike girls, boys are not conditioned to express their deep feelings or vulnerability. A guy who cries is quickly labeled a "wuss." After deeper probing, the psychological profiles of the young delinquents showed that they had been teased by other kids, or they had been rejected by a girlfriend. Since feeling bad or crying is a no-no, the only emotion in our culture that is acceptable to "being a man" is anger. Anger can be displayed in such ways as possessiveness, hostility, aggression, and insensitivity. Other behaviors are not as obvious, but still stem from anger. Guys can be withdrawn and uncommunicative. They can be cheap or nasty. Or they'll be bad boys, continuously getting into trouble. Or control freaks. Or liars. Angry guys may show a host of unacceptable traits that girls should stay away from. The questions are, "Do you heed the obvious warnings?" "Do you split from a guy who has shown you little respect?" "Or do you stick around, hoping to change him?"

Of course, not all guys are afraid to show compassion. The sensitive ones who demonstrate their feelings will be the ones who make the best boyfriends. Unfortunately, except for watching out for signs of obvious danger, *most girls have never been taught to be discriminating enough.* They have never learned that (a) they have choices, (b) they deserve to find guys who are kind, communicative, and caring, and (c) if a guy continually disses them, it's not their job to try to reform him and make him better. In fact, if this is how he is, he will probably never change. Yet too many girls accept poor treatment and try to sway this guy to become more loving. Lots of luck!

A study of 15,000 girls age 13 to 20, conducted by *YM* magazine, found that the top reason girls choose to have sex is because of curiosity, not love. While more than 75 percent of the girls said it was important to be in love with a guy before having sex with him, only 58 percent of them said they were. Forty-five percent thought the guy loved them, 20 percent felt pressured, and almost half of those who became sexually active, most at age 15, said they were too young. Based on these findings, most nonvirginal teenage girls are sorry and disappointed that they didn't wait until the circumstances were more appropriate.

Because of the overwhelming number of my letters, e-mails, and discussions with teenage girls, because of the recent school killings in the news, and because there is nothing else around to help girls choose guys who won't hurt them, I realized that I had to write this book. There is just too much teen unhappiness with relationships that don't work.

The aim of this book is to show girls how to protect themselves from the not-so-good guys. By protection, I don't mean using condoms and other birth control methods. But what I do mean is that, although it is important to consider birth control and other issues if a girl chooses to have sex, girls must also learn to protect themselves emotionally so they can keep the amount of hurt they suffer to a minimum. Most girls are obsessed with having a boyfriend. I'm not about to lecture on the rights and wrongs of this obsession, because you already know about it. But this book will teach you how to calm down long enough to attract someone who won't give you grief, someone who is worthy of the effort and caring you put into making your relationship solid.

Unfortunately, most of you don't realize how much power girls have. Several studies prove that girls are emotionally sturdier than boys, and that their healthy development is most harmed when they are restricted or confined. Yet you often long to confine yourself to one steady boyfriend, believing he will be the answer to all your prayers. I will show you why you should give up that idea. Instead, I'll teach you to develop your own skills and pursue your education so you'll have the know-how to find fulfilling relationships. Girls who understand and apply their power avoid setting themselves up to be victims of pain. They know how to stay away from the wrong guys. From this book, you'll learn that love doesn't have to hurt.

Love with the right guy can be supportive, entertaining, exciting, and wonderful. But for it to be all those things, you've got to realize that guys aren't *all that*. When I told my 15-year-old niece the title of the book, she laughed. When I told her the subtitle: "How to Attract the *Good* Guys," she said, "That's a great subtitle because good guys are so hard to find."

The Spice Girls sent a message to the world about "girl power." Now it's time for every girl to realize that before she gives a guy credit for being hot (especially if he's not), she should celebrate her own uniqueness. In this book, you'll recognize that you are the real Number One—and that number must never change.

From all the experience I've had dealing with teens, I know that girls need to hear this information straight up. A lot of girls sit on their own feelings as they put up with poor treatment from guys. You know that you'd never accept this kind of abuse from your girlfriends. But with guys, your aim is usually not to rock the boat. You don't want a guy to think you're too much trouble. Adult women often do the same dumb thing. Instead of confronting a guy and causing a commotion, they suffer from the "Duh Factor" and accept things as they are. Then they are miserable—and they write to me.

Look at these two letters. One is from a grown woman and the other is from a teenage girl. Notice how eerily similar they are.

Dear Dr. Gilda:

I'm a 52-year-old woman, in love with Tom, who's 62. We have a "committed" relationship, which, in his mind, means he doesn't sleep with anyone but me. But he escorts female "friends" to various social events and flirts with women constantly, right in front of my eyes. I'm furious that he doesn't take our relationship as seriously as I do. I feel disrespected and humiliated. One guy I know saw Tom with one of his female "friends," figured he and I had broken up, and asked me out. Although I've told Tom how I feel, he has not changed his behavior. What should I do?   *Carol*

Dear Dr. Gilda:

I'm 14 and I've been dating Jon for two months. After a few weeks of knowing each other, I was starting to fall for him more than any other boy. Last week we got into a big fight about him flirting with other girls and asking them to have sex with him. When I told him I was angry, he said, "Oh, honey, you know I love you and when I say that stuff I'm not serious." So I believed him. Finally, one day at school he was being really mean to me, not waiting for me where we usually meet, ditching me to walk off with my best friend, and telling me on the phone how hot she is. I've been crying myself to sleep for a week. What should I do?   *Janice*

There is almost 40 years' difference between these two gals. Both are miserable because they thought they had an exclusive relationship—only to discover that the guy had a different meaning for the term than they did. What is the problem here? Why are girls experiencing the sort of disappointment with their boyfriends that doesn't change once they meet supposedly mature men? Is there something you can do that will teach you how to prevent being hurt so that when you are adult women you won't experience the same pain? The answer is YES. You *can* learn the skills to ward off bad treatment as soon as it occurs. In fact, if you learn to be more discriminating about who you fall for while you're young, you may be able to avoid the painful separations and divorces that often come when you're older. The technique is called Taking Care of Number One. Traditionally, females are not good at their own caretaking because they've been taught to be the caretakers of others, not only *first,* but often *instead of,* themselves. Women who give too much get stressed, burned out, and angry that no one is there for them in their hour of need.

From now on, recognize that you've got only one person to nurture above all others—YOU. People who don't know better may call you "selfish." The word *selfish* seems to be used for gals who take care of their own needs at the expense of others. But that's nonsense. Being *self*ish is far better than being self*less,* meaning having no self. Selflessness means your needs get put on the back burner and eventually fall off the stove. So here selfishness is defined as self-protection, as though you are putting a protective shield around yourself. Self-protection is the only technique that makes sense because, let face it:

Gilda Gram   If you don't protect yourself, who will?

Gilda Grams, like the one above, are feel-good statements that you can repeat and write down when you're bummed or when you want a boost. These are important points I have made throughout the book that will be easy for you to pinpoint and remember. When you say them or write them, they'll quickly improve your mood. Gilda Grams will also give you a push to follow your own dreams while the guys you know are off doing whatever it is guys do when they're not with girls.

In the next chapters, you will learn what girls *want* and what girls *need*. What people *want* is what they'd *like to have*. What they *need* is what they *have to have*. From the letters I've received and the counseling I've done with teenage girls, I've found that the two things they *want* most in their social life are: 1) loyal girlfriends and 2) a cool boyfriend. But to get what you want and to be sure that the girlfriends and boyfriends you get stay with you, you *need* to know about things that you may think are totally unrelated to girlfriends and boyfriends. These things are found in the 4 Secrets of Love, and they consist of four honest-to-goodness needs:

1. You *need* to have and project self-confidence
2. You *need* to understand what makes guys tick
3. You *need* to be able to create your own excitement
4. You *need* to nurture your male friendships before pressuring a particular boy for a commitment.

Notice that loyal girlfriends and a cool boyfriend are all *external* to who you are as a human being. The crazy and ironic thing about being a *competent* person is that a girl must first become a *confident* person. Personal confidence makes social life a lot smoother and safer. With 11-year-olds, experts found that confidence is a good shield against bullying. Kids who showed confidence were not picked on as often because they projected their worth in their ability to defend themselves. And researchers in Finland studied 16,410 kids in high school, age 14 to 16. Surprisingly, they found that, believe it or not, those who were considered the bullies were often depressed, and they contemplated suicide more often than other kids.

Notice that the four needs listed above are *your* personal needs—for example, *your* need for self-confidence, *your* need for understanding, *your* need to be creative, and *your* need to nurture. Your needs belong to you alone, not to the girlfriends and boyfriends who hang out with you.

When girls don't respect their own needs they attract girlfriends who are jealous and boyfriends who are lame. The premise of this book is that when guys and other girls see how much you respect yourself, you'll attract the people who support that respect. The rule is simple:

Gilda Gram   We attract people who are like us.

Follow the guidelines in this book and become the best you can be so you'll attract the best there is out there.

PART I

What Girls *Want*

2 Hits to Happiness

WANT #1

Loyal Girlfriends

d o you remember how Linda Tripp taped Monica Lewinsky's personal and private conversations with her, and then played them back for the whole world to hear? Females around the world were appalled that a so-called "friend" would do such an evil thing. Every female alive knows what a sacred bond it is to confide in a special friend. Most of us have had the painful experience of trusting someone we thought was a friend with a secret, and then hearing our private information blabbed about behind our back.

Interestingly, when a female bonobo chimpanzee gets unwanted sexual attention from one of the males, she sounds a distress call and her female buddies come running to her rescue. In this species, the females are the law enforcers. The strong bonds they maintain with other females defend them against troublemaking males.

The same kind of bonding exists with loyal girlfriends. Yet sometimes there is interference, and what was once a great friendship can fall apart at the seams—unless the parties aggressively take action. This is what happened with Gail and her friends, all of whom lived in a nice community in Maryland. One of their good guy friends, Greg, moved to South Carolina because his father had been transferred in his job. Since they were all so close, whenever Greg had a school break, he returned to his old neighborhood to visit. Usually, he stayed at his best friend Cindy's house. On one Friday night, Cindy took Greg to a party. While he was there, he hooked up with Rosemarie. When he returned to Cindy's house, he noticed that she was decidedly cool. He asked her what was wrong, but she blankly said, "Nothing." Instead, the next day being Saturday and no school, she got on the phone with Rosemarie and confessed that she really liked Greg, but she had just never told him. She told Rosemarie that she was angry at her for hooking up with him under her nose. Rosemarie became angry herself, telling Cindy that if she had only known that she liked Greg, she would have considered him "off limits" and she would have stayed clear.

When Monday came, two other girls at the party, Andrea and Holly, were deep in conversation over Greg. Andrea told Holly that Greg was coming from South Carolina to visit her during the coming weekend. Rosemarie got wind of this and became furious, not with Andrea for snatching the guy she laid claim to, but with Holly! Getting angry at Holly instead of Andrea made sense to Rosemarie because she was afraid of getting into a dispute with Andrea, the school big-mouth. Rosemarie thought it was safer to lodge her anger against her friend, Holly. But when Holly got wind of Rose-marie's anger toward her, she, in turn, got angry with Rose-marie for being angry with her. Suddenly, everyone was fighting over one guy.

Rosemarie and Holly were good friends. They saw that things had gotten out of control. They decided to take a deep breath as each retold her side of the story. They both admitted that since Andrea is such a gossip, neither of them wanted to get in her face. Each one agreed that she could be a "really, really big bitch" and they didn't want her to turn other girls against them. They decided to do more digging—only to find out that Andrea had told them a lie. Greg had no intention of coming to Maryland to see her. Besides, everyone knew that when he visited his old neighborhood, it was Cindy he always stayed with—and now that Cindy had a secret crush on Greg, who didn't return her feelings, it was doubtful that she would invite him for a while. After every-thing was over, both girls were relieved that they had not fallen into the trap of allowing another girl, and a liar as well, to alter their relationship. These girls were smart enough to end their grief before they allowed Andrea to create a rift between them.

While guys usually play sports or perform other physical activities in groups, and brag about their success to each other, girls relate differently. We cherish our friendships above most other things, and we'd like to believe we can count on our friends to protect our confidential information and reputations. Friends offer a special brand of emotional connection that guys never experience with their buddies. For girls, friends are the sounding boards who reflect what is right or wrong, good or bad, moral or immoral. From their friends' responses, they get a sense of who they are and who they will become. When an intruder—such as Andrea— tries to come between them, girls must bond even more closely.

Most girls feel better after discussing their parents, school, other girls, or guys with their friends. Even before a girl notices that guys are on the planet, she invests her time and emotions in her friends, often setting aside regular phone time just to gab. Thirteen-year-old Laurie observed that before high school her focus was on family, friends, and school—in that order. But once she got to high school, her focus changed to friends as first in importance, school next, and family last. Yes, friends are very important as girls start to grow.

When a girl becomes boy-obsessed, it's her friends who enjoy every detail of each crush. During a romance, a girl's friends are there to help her figure out what the guy's actions *really* mean. (Unless, of course, a girl is so involved with her guy that she drops her friends altogether—which a lot of girls do, until they learn that boys can never replace the enduring friendships that girlfriends offer.) When a girl breaks up with a guy, it's her friends who make her feel better and shield her from the pain the fool caused her. When she's between guys, her friends go out with her to search for new ones. But when a friend suddenly backstabs her, it's probably more upsetting than if it had been a guy who had done it. And that's when she draws upon her other friends to make her feel better about having been turned on by "that bitch."

Since friendships help you discriminate between good and evil, they provide important links to reality. Most important, the finding and keeping of girlfriends is good training before hooking up with guys. The added bonus is that the way to deal with girlfriends follows the same game plan as the way to deal with guys. So if you master how to deal with the ups and downs of female friendships, you'll be able to avoid making fatal flaws later when you have to deal with that other gender.

All relationships—whether with girls or guys—draw from two parts of your personality: 1) your inner self and 2) your outer self. Your inner self is where you spend time alone, pursue special interests, and enjoy who you are as an individual. It is the place where you do your deepest thinking and have personal conversations with yourself that only you know about. Your outer self is where you enjoy support and encouragement from other people, namely your friends, that you can't get when you're alone. Friendships are outside your inner and private world, and they are meant to build on the inner self that you've already established. In other words:

Gilda Gram

Friendships should *enhance* your already strong inner self.

If your friends gossip about you behind your back, put you down, criticize you, and make you feel bad, they are not enhancing your inner self. To enhance who you already are, friends should build you up, encourage you to pursue your dreams, and give you a general feeling of joy to be around them. Overall, they should be able to do more for you when you're with them than you can do for yourself when you're alone.

Even if you've had a friend for a long time with whom you have closely bonded, other people, events, and things often get in the way. For example, a new girl moves into your class and you find that you want to spend more time with her than with your best friend. Or your parents have you on early curfew, but your friend's folks think it's okay for her to stay out till midnight. Or your friend has hooked up with a new guy, she's always with him, and you feel as though you've been put out in the cold. These changes that crop up from time to time can cause rifts between you and a friend even after you've been together for many years. Changing your friendships might not feel comfortable, but in reality, it's a fact of life. Changing our likes, our wants, and our tastes is all part of the way we grow. Consider this: When you are 22, you don't want to still think as you did when you were 12, right?

Even though people change and develop continually, friendships must be nurtured by *both* friends in order to last. If two people want to get together, they must deliberately create time for each other even through the distractions. If their schedules are packed, they will need to arrange times in advance to see each other so that they can enjoy the activities they once did. For friendships to last, both people have to reach out.

Do you consider yourself a good friend? For each of the following situations, which of the three responses would you choose?

HOW GOOD A FRIEND ARE YOU?

1. Marney is crushing on a new guy who just moved to her school. She and Beth have been best friends for six years, but now Marney is acting boy-crazy, following this guy around, bumping into him at his locker, and staring at him like a deer caught in the headlights of an oncoming car. Beth thinks Marney's making a fool of herself. She:

____✓ **a)** levels with Marney about how foolish she looks, and recommends other ways of getting this guy's attention.

_____**b)** goes along with and encourages Marney's silly behavior because she doesn't want to destroy their friendship.

_____**c)** admits to herself that Marney is acting ridiculous, does not want any part of it, and ends the friendship with a simple "See ya."

2. Carolyn has just become interested in watching basketball, a passion that her best friend, Janette, doesn't share. Carolyn begins to go to their school's basketball games, hangs out with other basketball fans, and seems to be generally drifting away from the close friendship the two have shared for three years. Janette is hurt that Carolyn has almost totally dropped her, and she tells Carolyn that she's upset. Carolyn:

_____✓ a) admits she's been distracted by her new passion. She apologizes to Janette, and asks her to join them at the next basketball game, telling her she doesn't want to end their friendship. When Janette declines to go, Carolyn suggests doing something else together.

_____ b) tells Janette that she's willing to forgo attending the next game so she can be with Janette.

_____ c) says, "Tough! You and I have different interests now and I don't think we have much in common anymore." She completely drops their friendship.

3. Millie is in the library studying for her next final when she overhears her best friend, Sara, giggling to another girl that Millie is too immature and ugly to attract a guy. Millie had considered Sara to be a supportive best friend, so she's shocked to hear her backstabbing. Millie:

_____ a) rises from her study carrel and looks straight into Sara's eyes, thereby letting her know that she heard everything and she's pissed. She need not say another word.

_____✓ b) rises from her study carrel and screams at Sara that she's a two-faced bitch who can't be trusted.

_____c) ignores the incident, deciding that Sara is so popular that it pays for her to continue the friendship despite the fact that Sara is two-faced.

4. Maureen has just started smoking cigarettes and pot. Now she's pressuring her best friend, Kris, to do the same. Kris is on the swimming team and knows how detrimental smoking can be to her athletic performance. Yet she's torn because Maureen has been a great friend and she doesn't want to lose her. Kris:

_____✓ a) levels with Maureen and tells her, "Sorry, smoking is just not for me."

_____b) lies that her uncle had lung cancer and she made a promise to her mother that she would never put any kind of smoke into her lungs.

_____c) gives in just to continue to be in Maureen's popular crowd.

5. A new girl has just moved next door to Meri. It hasn't taken her long to get tight with the "fast" crowd, which Meri's mom has observed. In fact, Meri's mother has forbidden Meri to get friendly with this girl. The new girl is assigned to the seat next to Meri in math class. When they bump into each other outside their homes, the girl asks Meri to leave her test paper uncovered tomorrow during their final exam so she can copy her answers. Meri:

_____✓____a) tells her mom and opens an honest discussion with her about the best way to handle this dilemma. The next day, she tells the new girl that she doesn't want to get into trouble for cheating.

_____b) says okay so that she doesn't make an enemy of this "fast" girl or her friends.

_____c) stays home from school on the day of the test.

Score Card

Take 20 points for each (a); 10 points for each (b); 5 points for each (c).

Analysis

75–100: Your friends can count on your loyalty. Whatever you're doing, keep it going.

50–75: Be stronger in sticking by your values instead of being swayed by those of your friends. Make your values your priority regardless of what your friends say.

25–50: You need to be forthright about your feelings. Your beliefs are your own special brand of who you are.

The 5 Rules of Friendship

On that big day that you go to take the test for your driver's license, you know how hard you worked in preparation to passing the exam. You've studied the driver's manual, learned the rules of the road, and practiced hours of driving with your instructor. When the time comes, you're elated when you pass with flying colors.

Keeping friends is just as important as passing a driving test, yet no one has ever given us rules on how to behave when we're involved in a friendship. When a friendship "crashes," there is no insurance policy that will pay our emotional bills. Somehow, we have to get by—with poor preparation and little guidance. When these relationships break up, there's no getting around it: we get hurt. Friends are people we love, and no one wants to see her friendships end. There are ways of preserving our relationships with the people we care about before we take the final action of walking out.

What follows are real letters from girls in conflict who asked for my advice about their relationship issues. Little did they know that many of their issues with friends can be solved by following the 5 Rules of Friendship:

1. Don't let guys come between you.
2. Schedule specific time for your friends.
3. If a friend backstabs you, confront her in a way she will hear.
4. If a friend pressures you to do things you're not comfortable with, stand your ground.
5. Share your friendship issues with your parents.

Rule #1: Don't Let Guys Come Between You

When guys come between two best friends, a friendship that has lasted years could derail.

Dear Dr. Gilda:

I have a major problem. My two best friends and I are in the biggest fight of our lives! Blair and I have been best friends since second grade. We've been through everything from crushes to thoughts of suicide. Keegan and I met last year. I fell in love with him but we stayed just friends. Last month, Keegan and I had an extra-credit project so he came over to my house. Next thing I knew we were making out. I told two people, Blair and one other girl (it totally slipped out). Well, somehow or other Keegan's best boy bud found out and was teasing him. Keegan totally blew up at me (which I totally understand and I've already apologized enough). But to get back at me, he started flirting with Blair, who actually flirted back with him!! I know Blair's liked him forever but I was the one who liked him first and I was also the one who introduced them. I hate her now and won't even talk to her. She didn't even apologize for making a jackass of herself. I still want Keegan for a friend. What do I do??

Sad but Also Mad, 16 years old

Dear Sad but Also Mad:

This is a major problem because you trusted both these people and now they've turned on you. That stinks—and it makes you wonder who you can trust, especially in the future. Girls should always follow my rule of never letting a guy come between them. What's up with Blair that she's so desperate for a guy? Or does she admire you so much that she wants what you have—even if it means your boyfriend? For friends who have been together since second grade, she sure has shown a lapse of judgment. And no one can blame you for feeling that you hate her now. But you have been best friends for a long time. Would you feel comfortable having a heart-to-heart with her, telling her how you feel? Maybe she'll hear how hurt you are and see the error of her ways. Then again, if she doesn't, you're better off without her. Friends need to be trustworthy.

As for Keegan, you should admit that you understand how embarrassed he was because of your wagging (or bragging?) tongue. Guys don't like to be embarrassed in front of their friends, especially when it comes to mushy romance. You can continue to apologize to him for your own lapse of judgment and see if he will forgive you. Truthfully, he may be too off the wall with discomfort to talk to you for a long time.

Most important, I hope you've learned your lesson about talking too much about your personal business. Please let me know what happens after you try to put out these fires.

Dr. Gilda

Even after a romance has ended, wanting to go out with a best friend's ex could still present a sticky situation:

Dear Dr. Gilda:

My best friend told me that she likes my ex-boyfriend and wouldn't mind going out with him. He dumped me six months ago and I'm still not over him. I would definitely have a problem with them going out. Am I being selfish?   *NJ, 16*

Dear NJ:

If this girl were a casual acquaintance who didn't know the score about your feelings for this guy, I'd say that you can't fault her. But this is your *best friend*. Look who's really the selfish one! I have a simple rule for dating exes of best friends: best friends can share crises, clothes, and comments. But they should never share boyfriends. Maybe if you were completely over him, you'd feel differently about the two of them together at this time. But you're not—and she knows it—so she ought to be more sensitive to your feelings. Tell her just that—and also let her know how disappointed in her you are for even raising the question. Of course, she'll go ahead and do whatever she wants to do anyway. But after you confront her, her actions will tell you whether you want to keep her around as a friend in the future.   *Dr. Gilda*

When girls let guys get between their friendship, there are many hurt feelings and broken relationships. Since friends have a lot in common, it's not unusual for two friends to like the same guy. But usually, the one who liked him first is the one who lays claim to him, while the other one dutifully respects her friend's likes. Most girls follow this "unwritten" agreement—meaning no one ever speaks about it—but because it is unwritten, there are often lots of problems when one girl decides that it's open season on another girl's man. This is how one twosome worked it out.

Throughout her years in school, Ellen, now 14, had had about ten different boyfriends, so she was aware that boys would come and go in and out of her life. During Christmas break, a group of Ellen's girlfriends decided to go skating at their local ice skating rink. The only drawback to these plans was that Ellen's best friend, Katrina, couldn't come because of a bad cold. But Ellen went anyway with five other girls. As she skated around the rink, falling and flopping with her giddy girlfriends, one of the guys from school came up to her. In fact, as she was slipping on the ice for the umpteenth time, Jeff held her up so she didn't land facedown. She and Jeff began to skate around the rink for about an hour, laughing and joking at all the other skaters who weren't as lucky to have Jeff by their side to prevent them from falling. As she was leaving, Ellen realized that she really liked Jeff. However, she also recognized that this presented a dilemma for her because her friend Katrina was already going out with him. She didn't dare share this information with her best friend, even though they always discussed *everything*. Instead, Ellen held her feelings inside, and felt somewhat guilty for having them. But she remembered when another boy had tried to come between the two of them and almost ruined their friendship. Now she was determined to stick to the rule that she and Katrina had made up after that event: "Chicks before dicks." Being a trustworthy friend, Ellen honored their agreement and went on to like someone else. "Jeff is so out of the picture now," she said recently. "These days I like Sean." How many girls would have packed in a romance with a cute guy their friend liked?

Not everyone chooses to solve their common loves so maturely. Morgan and her best friend seem to enjoy playing musical chairs with guys, and for them it's all right to exchange boyfriends:

Dear Dr. Gilda:

I hope you can help me. You see, I have this crush on this guy, but he's my best friend's ex, and he still loves her. He's not very cute, but he's really nice. Well, my best friend likes him too, but she's already got a DORKY, FREAKISH, JERKY, UGLY, NASTY, OBNOXIOUS BONEHEAD of a boyfriend. He's my ex . . . unfortunately. Well, I really like my best friend's ex a lot. He's sending mixed signals to me. I dunno what to do. Please help me.   *Morgan*

Dear Morgan:

In this case, I'm concerned that you are crushing on someone who still loves someone else. Are there only two guys in your town? Why are you willing to take your friend's cast-offs? Usually, I aim to protect the feelings of the girl whose best friend runs off with her man. But it seems not to bother either of you that you exchange guys as you would recipes. So, if it's okay with both of you, it's fine with me.

Yet you're setting yourself up for heartache if you already know that he's still devoted to your friend. Could you possibly be trying to get back at her for running off with your ex? When you believe you deserve more than crumbs, you will decide what you want from a relationship and go for someone who's truly available. Love should never entail a Ping-Pong game of does he/doesn't he want me! *Dr. Gilda*

Each case is different, and every girl has a different feeling about whether it's okay for her friends to date her ex. For some it doesn't matter, but for others, the wounds cut deep. To prevent unnecessary conflicts, you should know in advance how your friends feel on this issue.

No matter who she chooses to love, each girl deserves to be cherished for the special person she is. She can be cherished by her girlfriends as well as by her guy. The only thing to remember is that one relationship should not get in the way of another. Even in the case of Morgan liking her best friend's ex, there would never be a potential conflict if she chose to like a guy who has not gone out with any of her friends. *Do you hear what I'm saying??*

Rule #2: Schedule Specific Time for Your Friends

Everyone is so busy these days that it's easy to find yourself drifting away from the friends you had once spent a lot of time with. Often, as girls are growing, they develop other interests that lead them to want to hang out with different groups of people. This can be very hurtful for the friends they leave behind, as you can see in the following letter:

Dear Dr. Gilda:

Alicia and I started hanging out together at the beginning of the year. Then this girl she knew from a few years ago started hanging out with her. This new person began dragging her everywhere and she won't hang out with me anymore. I want to tell Alicia how I feel, but I can never get her alone. I also have no one else to hang with. Will Alicia ever realize I want to hang with her, and if not, how do I tell her?   *Louise*

Dear Louise:

Obviously you're hurting badly because Alicia has left you flat for someone else. Being left flat wouldn't make anyone feel good. But what makes your predicament especially painful is that Alicia seems to be your only friend. That is a dangerous situation to put yourself in because, as you have seen, if something happens to your friendship, you are left with an emptiness caused by having no one at all. The way to protect yourself from feeling alone is to have one or two *great* friends, but also to cultivate other friends as well. These others may not be quite as close to you as your best friends are, but you can still enjoy being with them when you want to have some fun.

Instead of spending your energy worrying about whether Alicia will or won't realize you want to still hang with her, invest your time in finding more friends. Get into the things you love to do and see how many people you attract who enjoy the same things you do.

Dr. Gilda

It's a fact of life that people grow, move away, and move on to other interests and other people. While most girls like to have one or two *best* friends, having other friends as well is a smart thing. Try to keep as many of your friendships as alive as possible. That means specifically arranging time to be with them, or at least talking to them on the phone or by e-mail. Because many of your friends may belong to different groups, you might try mixing friends from one group with friends from another. This way, you won't feel like you have to choose all the time. Of course, it's possible that people from one group won't like the people from another, and then you'll have to make some decisions each time you want to hang out. If this happens, level with your old friends and tell them that you don't want to lose them. Let them make some suggestions about how to fix the problem. But understand, sometimes friends do grow apart because they no longer share the same interests. If that's the case, accept it as a fact of life and move on gracefully. Know that you'll soon attract people who are more in line with your own values and tastes.

Rule #3: If a Friend Backstabs You, Confront Her in a Way She Will Hear

Nobody deserves a friend who is two-faced and can't be trusted. Friends are supposed to support you whether it's to your face or behind your back. Sometimes a friend we've trusted becomes jealous or nasty or whatever—and we become not only disappointed, but angry that this person has turned on us. The question is always, "Should I confront the friend who backstabbed me? And if so, how?"

There's a rule I suggest for confronting anyone who has hurt you. Ask the question, "Will I be dealing with this person again?" If she's someone you'll never see again, or at least will see rarely, forget it—and her. But if she's someone you will continue to run into at school or in your neighborhood, or if she still hangs with your best buds, or if you have some classes in common, you might want to clear the air to let her know you heard her negative comments about you and you're less than pleased. But you will not want to say it in a way that will make her defensive. If you act too accusatory, she'll only come back with, "No, I didn't" or "You don't know what you're talking about." Instead, it's best to be direct and honest in your confrontation.

Successful Confrontation

Before you decide to tell someone off, you must decide what you want to accomplish with your confrontation. If you scream, yell, and curse at her, all she may hear is your angry temper. Her response may be to come back at you with similar screaming, yelling, and cursing. A catfight is not exactly what you need. Instead, you'll want to be honestly up front with her about how you feel in a way that she will hear.

How do you have a successful confrontation? There are just 3 steps you need to remember. They are:

1. "When you said (or did) . . . ,
2. I felt . . ."
3. Stop.

The last step, or Stop, is a separate step, because steps 1 and 2 are so powerful that the person you're confronting will probably suddenly listen to how what she did affected the way you *felt*. No normal person wants to be the one accused of hurting someone. Because your listener is suddenly hearing you, maybe even for the first time, you might be tempted to tell her about *all* the times you felt awful as a result of her behavior. Instead, follow the Stop sign, and put a lid on it. This is one of those cases where less is more.

After your confrontation, your so-called friend might feel really bad or embarrassed. She may try to offer some lame excuse, which will probably be some lie like, "I never did that," or "Tom didn't really understand what I was saying when he said that I said that." It doesn't matter what this chick's comeback is. What does matter is that you got your grief off your chest and now she's left with egg on her face and in need of a Handi Wipe. Too bad! Let her somehow try to slither her way out of it.

Confrontation is not the most comfortable thing in the world. But this technique is more for you than it is for your friend, because when you let her know you're on to her, you take total control. So confrontation has two main benefits: 1) it lets your friend know that you will not allow anyone to parade as a friend and then turn on you when you're not looking, and 2) it teaches you how to stick up for yourself so that no one in your future will be able to get away with trashing you. These are important lessons to learn no matter who is in your life.

What you decide to do after you have heard your friend's excuses is up to you. You might want to give her a second chance to prove herself (and you better believe that if she wants to keep you as a friend, she'll now be on her best behavior), or you might want to permanently ditch the two-faced foe. It really doesn't matter what you decide because now you're in control—and everyone around you will know it. Enjoy your newfound power!

Now that you know to successfully confront someone, how would you handle this sticky situation?

> *Dear Dr. Gilda:*
>
> I visited my family in another state over Christmas vacation. When I came back, my best friend said that she slept with my boyfriend while I was gone. He swears that nothing happened. And the other people who were at the party where this supposedly happened are saying that nothing happened between them. What do I do about this problem? HELP!!
> *S. S., age 17*

Before you hear my solution, take a minute to think about how you would respond. Put yourself in this girl's shoes. What would you do? Take into account that it's her best friend who has said this, and she probably sees her every day at school. If you remember the story about Rosemarie and Holly, who didn't want to get on big-mouthed Andrea's bad side, imagine what would happen if S. S.'s best friend is a gossip like Andrea. Why else would she spread a rumor like this about her supposedly best friend? Here's what I told S. S.:

> *Dear S. S.:*
>
> First of all, what kind of "best" friend do you have? Why would she even say this to you—much less do such a thing—if it really occurred? This so-called friend is obviously looking to hurt your feelings. If her tale is true, of course, you must dump her. But even if it's false and she's making it up, the question is WHY does she

want to make you suffer? Nobody needs friends who try to hurt their feelings.

Look for signs from your boyfriend to determine if his feelings for you have changed in any way. Forget about what the other people at the party said, unless they were acting as his bodyguard during the entire night. A relationship is between you and your boyfriend, not between you, your boyfriend, and others. The basis of every relationship has got to be trust. You deserve to be respected, by both your girlfriends and your boyfriend.

You surely are not getting respect from your girlfriend. But if you find out you're also not getting what you deserve from your guy, it's time to move on. Just imagine what life will be like when you have girlfriends and a boyfriend whom you can trust and who respect and support you.

Dr. Gilda

Having a "best friend" who would want to compete with a girl for her boyfriend's attentions, even if what she said was true, is too much hurt to bear. Being cheated on by her boyfriend would make any girl feel awful. We don't really know if that's the case. But besides having a guy who cheats on you, nobody needs to have a two-timing best friend as well.

As far as best friends go, the only question remaining is whether S. S. feels the need to confront her "friend." Will she be running into her again? If so, how frequently? How will she feel when she sees her? If S. S. feels the need to set the record straight and tell her how she feels, then confrontation is the way to go.

Rule #4: If She's Pressuring You to Do Things You're Not Comfortable with, Stand Your Ground

Sometimes your good friends will drink, smoke, use drugs, or do slutty things. They may be experimenting with new activities, or they could be acting out new behaviors they intend to keep. Any of these behaviors may not sit well with you, but that doesn't necessarily mean that you should drop these people from your roster of pals. The challenging part of growing up is knowing that:

Gilda Gram   Life is about making choices.

Sometimes you must choose to stick up for your values. Other times you must decide to utter that difficult word, "no," to the pressures your friends are foisting on you. This is not to say that the pressures you feel are not real. According to a survey by Peter D. Hart Research Associates, teen pressures include getting good grades, getting into college, fitting in socially, and using drugs and alcohol. Saying no to any or all of these takes a lot of courage. No matter what you choose to do, understand that it is ultimately *your choice*—not anyone else's—to decide what is right for you. Choosing is not only your right, but your obligation because:

Gilda Gram	It is only you who will suffer the consequences of your actions.

Being a good friend suggests that after you've chosen the right course of action for yourself, you will want to "spread the gospel" in a positive way. For example, if you see that a friend is going down the wrong path, being a supportive friend yourself, you may want to advise her about some of the consequences of her behavior, as these girls wanted to do with their friend:

Dear Dr. Gilda:

We're 13 and our best friend is 12, and she is, well, put it this way, not a virgin!! She has had sex and does several other things that 12-year-olds should not be doing! Every time she goes out with someone, she tries to get him in bed. All her friends are telling her she shouldn't be doing things like that at her age, but she says she loves these boys. We know she doesn't know what love is. What should we do?

Her concerned friends,
Sherry and Cassie

Dear Sherry and Cassie:

First of all, you girls are making a judgment call. There could be any number of reasons you may decide that your friend's behavior does not match yours, and people make judgments about one another all the time. You girls are doing the right thing by advising your promiscuous friend about the consequences of her behavior. She may not like you butting into her life and business, and this could be the beginning of the parting of your ways, because one thing friends share is common values. You guys, in fact, may choose not to hang out with her anymore because people are often judged by the company they keep, and if your friend's behavior is slutty and she won't listen to your advice, you may not want to be judged as slutty, too. This is up to you.

The most important thing about whether or not you decide to keep this girl as a friend is whether you feel pressure from her to do the same kinds of things she's doing. If you do, you must stand your ground. Nobody should pressure anyone into any kind of behavior that makes her feel uncomfortable. So make your pitch to your friend, check out her reactions, and then decide if it's worth the consequences for you to remain in her circle.

Dr. Gilda

Girls need to develop a strong inner self so that they will feel comfortable making the right choices. Wherever you are and whatever you're doing, the question about values is always yours alone to decide. With a strong inner self, you will understand the consequences of bad behavior long after your so-called "friends" are gone. You'll be able to decide to do the right thing *for you*, even when you have to make a decision in a moment's notice.

When you choose to stand your ground, there is one warning. Sometimes sticking to your values can be lonely. If you choose an unpopular view, you may be pegged as a "rebel girl." Some of your friends might bad-mouth you and try to make you feel uncomfortable for not going along with them. If this is the case for you, recognize that, no matter what you choose to do,

Gilda Gram   Everyone is not always going to love you.

When you've mastered this Gilda Gram, you'll know that your inner self is getting very strong. You'll also know that you're ready to stand up for your views, no matter who objects.

Rule #5: Share Your Friendship Issues with Your Parents

According to *USA Today*'s teen panel of twenty-five members, growing up usually means growing away from your parents. In an effort to become independent, teens want less parental togetherness, and more time to spend with friends.

Consequently, parents feel isolated and cast aside. With that being more the rule than the exception, I don't often hear from a parent who actually appreciates the boyfriend her daughter has. In the following case, the parent has let *her* friends in on her daughter's circumstances, and they disagree with this mom's parenting. When I received this lovely note, I was quite impressed with this mother's togetherness:

Dear Dr. Gilda:

My 16-year-old daughter is in love with a sweet, wonderful, caring, generous man of 21. They have a great relationship, built on communication, respect, and trust. Due to their ages, I realize that the chances are that they will eventually drift apart. My friends think I'm crazy to allow them to be together. It would be possible for me to send him away, but my daughter is so much better off with him, so much happier and well adjusted, that I see no reason to do that.

He refuses to have intercourse, not because of her age, but because he wants to wait until he marries. They do engage in other sexual activities, though. My question is this: is it ever appropriate for a 16-year-old girl (she's not a virgin) and a 21-year-old man to be romantically involved?

Thanks so much for taking the time to read this.

Sincerely,

Jean Jones

Dear Jean:

Let me tell you that you seem to be one of the most level-headed parents I've heard from. When it comes to love, anything is possible. Of course, at 16, your daughter can't possibly know what she'll want when she's older. And even a man of 21 is not mature enough to map out his entire life's plan at this time. But since you recognize that they are good for each other, and since intercourse is not an issue, and there's no possibility of pregnancy or STDs, why can't this thing run its course?

Obviously, your daughter has experienced other sexual encounters before, yet she's in no hurry to press her boyfriend for sex now. I'd say you're doing the right thing in encouraging the romance to progress. You know where she is, you know with whom, you trust them both, and she'll either grow with him or take what she needs to learn from the experience and move on. If anything, your support of her choices does her a great amount of good. Unlike most girls her age, she won't get into the usual rebelliousness with you, because you haven't come down too hard on her.

I wish there were more rational moms out there like you. No wonder your daughter chose her man so wisely!

Dr. Gilda

Unlike this mom above, sometimes your parents won't like your friends for one reason or another and they will demand that you break off ties with them. Since you probably won't agree with their tastes and values, you'll end up begging and pleading for your folks to change their minds. Other times, a friend's parents may not like you for some reason. Then your friend will do the same thing with her parents to try to sway them to her way of thinking.

Dear Dr. Gilda:

I'm a 15-year-old girl with a huge problem. My best friend is Susan. Her parents hate me, and they won't let her be around me. I've talked to Susan about it but she says she can't stand up to her parents about it. I don't know why they hate me. I'm a good person and I know what I want in life. A couple of years ago, Susan and I were best friends, but we got into a terrible argument that included both sets of parents screaming at each other, and Susan and I didn't speak for a year. But now we're in the same classes, and we've become best friends again. Could parents hold a grudge that long? If not, then what's up?

Juliet

Dear Juliet:

Parents don't want to see their kids get hurt. In order to protect them, they set down rules that they believe will save their teens from pain. One of the rules that Susan's parents set down was meant to protect their daughter from getting into the same terrible situation again with you as she had in the past. Of course, both you girls believe you are older and wiser now that it's a year later, and that your parents should forget the past. Maybe yours have. But Susan's parents are still being protective of their daughter. That's natural.

Because of the bad history together you guys have, Susan should try to slowly reintroduce you to her parents as a new, mature friend. At the same time, she should level with her folks about some of the issues she is having in learning to trust you again. If she is honest with them, and open about trying to mend the past, chances are they will begin to see that their daughter is capable of making wiser decisions than she was a year ago. But this will take time, so be patient.   *Dr. Gilda*

Okay, let's get real here. No matter where your folks come from, no matter what their educational background or financial situation, they have one objective in mind: to protect their child—YOU—from hurt and harm. Therefore, understand that even if their perspective is based on their love for you:

Gilda Gram   Parents never give impartial advice.

Parents always have a hidden agenda, so recognize where they're coming from. If you get upset with their decisions about your life, keep in mind that they're acting in two roles—one, as your perhaps overprotective parents, and two, as your unpaid guardian angel. Sure, the first role can be a real pain, and their tastes might seem warped, but should you need the second one—and who doesn't need an angel occasionally?—look at what you've got as an added bonus.

Once again, you have some choices. You can reject the interference—as well as the benefits—from having concerned parents or you can let your folks in on your life and your choices so they can help you make tough decisions when you do need them. Your decision.

Sure you want to be independent. Sure you want to have your own life. Sure you want to break away. As you have already seen, making choices is a way of being a grown-up. And even grown-ups have to choose between two sticky possibilities that seem to be of equal importance. Choosing now is good training for your later years, when you'll need to choose between things that are far more important.

Girls who let their parents get to really know their friends have a better chance that their parents will trust their judgments. That translates to less hassle for you in the long run. Why? Because the more parents feel they know what's going on in their daughter's life, the more they'll trust that she's not trying to hide anything from them, and that she's safe. That mutual trust provides big payoffs. Sasha felt those payoffs after confiding in her mom about a tough relationship she was having with a girlfriend.

On the day she moved into Sasha's neighborhood, the new girl, Krissy, came to the school dance. Sasha saw that Krissy wore a slutty outfit that immediately won her acceptance into the popular crowd. Just a week later, Krissy confided to Sasha that she and another popular friend had stolen about $160 worth of merchandise from a local store. Sasha wanted to be in the popular crowd herself, but she knew that Krissy's actions were wrong. She told her mom about it, and her mom said she didn't want her to be friends with Krissy anymore. Sasha didn't know what to do because she still wanted acceptance by this popular crowd, which she didn't feel comfortable admitting to her mom. So she put off making her decision.

But then Krissy moved Sasha's decision along by acting bitchy toward her. This time, without hesitation, Sasha said good-bye. Now Sasha says she's glad she's not friends with Krissy anymore. She hears that she drinks, smokes, and gets into trouble all the time. Sasha believes that telling her mother was a good idea because it made her see the light, even if she didn't rush to follow her advice. Also, if she had been in Krissy's crowd, she might have tried doing some of the illegal things they were into, which she would have regretted later. Parents can make surprisingly good allies when you need them.

How Loyal Are Your Friends?

Now that you've assessed whether you're a good friend yourself, you're in a better position to judge the reliability of your friends toward you. Just as with guys, when we first meet new girlfriends, they are on their best behavior. If we trust too early in any relationship, we may let new "friends" in on some of our private secrets too soon, only to find that they gossiped behind our backs and hurt us. To be sure you know whether someone is really a good friend, take this Friendship Quiz:

FRIENDSHIP QUIZ

These are the names of five of my best buddies and the reasons I consider them to be loyal friends:

1.   because
2.   because
3.   because
4.   because
5.   because

Did you find that you were stumped on why you felt that any of these five friends were loyal? In other words, when it came to filling in the "because" part, did it take you a long time to think about why? If that's the case, it tells you that you must ask yourself more specific questions along the lines of the 5 Rules of Friendship:

1. Does your friend keep her scheduled dates with you even if a guy wants to see her?

2. Does she make time for you even though she has other friends?

3. If someone backstabs you, does she come to your defense?

4. Does she pressure you to do what she wants even when you're not interested and she knows it?

5. Are you comfortable filling your parents in on your friend's behavior, both good and bad?

What did you discover from your responses? Did you find that your so-called "friends" are often not there for you when you need them? Did you find that you were giving more than you were getting? It's your *choice* (here's that word again) either to follow the five rules we've outlined and reconsider who you want to keep around, or to rewrite friendship rules of your own. Remember, being picky between loyal and disloyal girlfriends is good training for the kind of treatment you'll eventually want and expect from a guy. This choosing process is called setting "boundaries" because it outlines the rules by which you need to live and love.

What Are Boundaries?

Boundaries are imaginary fences we place around ourselves. They are the silent rules we follow to determine what is okay and what is not when it comes to relating to other people. Boundaries are not meant to close people out. Instead, you construct them to conserve your energy and to respect your need for clear-thinking independence. Well-defined boundaries alert you when to say no and when to say yes. They advise you about who to hang out with. They instruct you to decline invitations when you have to study or when you're just too tired to go out. They tell you when you want to honor the need to stay home alone and just veg out.

The beauty of boundaries is that we draw these imaginary images in pencil so we can erase them and let certain people get closer. Because they are elastic, they allow us to expand our friendships when we've built a level of trust. The great thing about boundary building is that we do this without having to answer to anyone else. Boundaries are solely ours. They protect us. If we don't feel like getting too close to someone too quickly, it's okay, since we have decided to wait until we are ready to alter or expand the lines that we ourselves have created.

The learning experience you gain from setting boundaries with girlfriends is:

Gilda Gram

When you are comfortable setting boundaries with girlfriends, you'll be comfortable setting boundaries with guys.

So, think of your friendships with your girlfriends as learning experiences in how to deal with guys. Practice following the 5 Rules of Friendship, stick to your guns without backing down, and remember that you deserve to be treated well by everyone you meet.

WANT #2

A Cool Boyfriend

new product that just arrived on the market is a $3 pack of nine trading cards called "Boy Crazy!" It consists of pictures of cute boys along with some of their traits like age, eye color, horoscope sign, and the type of girls they prefer. There is a Web site that accompanies the cards, and on it girls register to vote for a boy of the week to host a live chat. Even before the cards became commercially available, 47,000 girls had already registered. There is no question that most teenage girls want to find a cool boyfriend. Yet why do girls have so many problems in achieving this goal? I believe it's because girls get a misconception of what life and love are all about from the children's books they are read when they are little.

Let's Dump the Fairy Tale Mentality

Remember the fairy tales that were read to you when you were a little girl? From so many stories, girls learned that love came as a result of waiting. Just think of Snow White and Sleeping Beauty, who met princes who were not quite "ready" for commitment. Their guys went off on journeys to seek adventure. Eventually they came home to the gals, who were, by then, either doing mindless housework with seven dwarfs, or deadened in a deep sleep. Of course, the girls did nothing productive while their guys were away. But miraculously, after the princes reappeared and either kissed or carried off the patient mistresses, everyone lived "happily ever after." Without saying it in actual words, these fairy tales implied, "Even though he's out partying, girls, your job is to wait around, go to sleep for a few years, and put any dreams you may personally have on hold. Your life will only count when *he* says it can."

Ho hum . . . Okay, we know that happily-ever-after doesn't exist. Just look at all the divorces around us! Even the best relationships have their ups and downs with problems that need to be worked through. These fairy tales, while entertaining, did girls a disservice. They taught that the most important thing in life for a girl is to find a "prince." To find him requires being a beautiful young thing who must wait to begin her life until after the prince returns from his own joyful romp. Or until he gets you to kiss him while he's in the form of a warty frog. Ugh! The idea of having to kiss some frogs before you find your prince is so widely accepted in our culture that it's permeated our books, movies, and cartoons. Even parents who have tried to raise their young daughters with a reality check still constantly run into this myth.

For example, my friend took her innocent four-year-old daughter on a camping trip with her older sister's Brownie troop. Before my friend knew it, little Melissa was holding a dirty little frog in the palm of her hand. My friend, who appreciates cleanliness, screamed, "Melissa, put that filthy thing down." But Melissa, raised to be an independent thinker, yelled, "No, Mom, I can't. I want to kiss this frog now so that he'll turn into a handsome prince." And with that she smacked one on the little creature. Gross! You would think this little girl would have realized that since the frog stayed a frog, the kiss idea was only make-believe. But Melissa went on and on the whole evening telling her mom that someday her prince would come!

Little girls who believe that a magical prince will find them and sweep them into a cloud of romance grow into teenagers and even adult women who believe that someday *their* prince will come. I've had 20-year-olds ask me, "You mean there's no Prince Charming?" Come on, girls. Guys are no more princes than girls are princesses. When we imagine that guys have royal qualities, we encourage them to think that they're more than human. We put them on a pedestal, allow them to treat us badly, and give in to pressures we don't need and can't handle. Like little Melissa, we think that the frog is a prince in disguise who will suddenly surprise us with love.

We need to dump our fairy tale mentality and get real. We need to see guys as they truly are—just guys. When we do that, we benefit in two ways:

1. We won't feel shy and uncomfortable about talking to guys because we'll know that they're just human beings like us. As human beings, they have the same insecurities and fears of looking stupid that girls do. When we see guys as our equals rather than as superhumans, we can relate to them just as we do to our other friends.

2. We won't allow them to make us feel bad because we'll know how to expect respect. When people are our real friends, they treat us well. Friends look out for each other. They go out of their way not to hurt our feelings. When we treat guys as our equals rather than as supermen, they give to us the kind of respect we give to them.

Gilda Gram   To have a cool boyfriend, dump the fairy tale mentality and get real.

Into the Millennium—with Still a Way to Go

Obviously, things little girls were learning had to change. Waiting around for something to happen for us is a big contrast to the take-charge Nike motto chanting, "Just Do It." In some ways, things did change, and it was for the better. Today young women recognize that they deserve to have dreams. They know they have a right to pursue them, and that they should strive to succeed. The more enlightened girls are finally getting a good education to put themselves in a position of becoming financially secure, meaning they don't have to depend on anyone else to support them. Women who are financially secure can be more choosy about the guys they select.

Yet, despite all the education about becoming financially independent, no matter how much money they're earning, too many girls still base their sole happiness on whether they have a guy. Look at Ally McBeal, the star character on one of the hottest shows on TV. Even though she has a law degree and a great job, her entire life revolves around trying to connect with a guy to get married and have babies. Translation: "Despite my scholastic accomplishments and my successful career, I'm still really nothing unless I have a man." With her gotta-get-a-husband attitude, it's a wonder she keeps her job! A lawyer in the real world, pulling her shenanigans, would not. But because of the popularity of this show, we see more and more girls identifying with Ally McBeal, despite the make-believe story lines, and (mis)believing that waiting for Prince Charming should be their greatest career goal.

Ally McBeal is not the only role model on TV that instructs girls that hooking up is the most important thing in life. Another media icon, Ally's younger guy-crazed "sister," is Felicity. She chooses to reject high-ranking Stanford University so she can follow her crush to a less prestigious New York City university. This is outrageous. College is where a girl will spend four years of her education supposedly improving herself. Not Felicity. As an incoming freshman, she majored in guy-chasing. What kind of role model of independence is this show for young girls leaving high school and seeking their future? As a very perceptive 17-year-old male confided to me, "Girls give up too much to be with guys." And girls should know that these guys don't respect them for it.

Any enlightened girl recognizes that in the real world, guys who are chased by needy chicks are just plain turned off. What we don't see on the screen is the reality that a girl's desperation to find a guy, get married, and have babies is as appealing to a guy as a cold shower. Desperation is probably the single most compelling force to make a guy flee fast in the opposite direction. If these are television's best role models for connecting, we are in deep trouble. Boyfriends come and go, but your dreams and goals and how you prepare to meet them are yours forever. Girls must acknowledge and stick to their dreams. Crush-craving should not be one of them. So, before you rush your crush, chill out. Instead,

Gilda Gram   You GOAL, girl.

And make your one main goal improving *yourself*, not snagging a boyfriend.

Love's Disappointments

Girls who have avoided pursuing their own passions are especially shattered when a guy leaves them. Angie is a 13-year-old in the eighth grade. As a pretty blond soccer player, she's probably the most popular girl in her school. She had been going with her boyfriend, Brian, for three months. Suddenly, one of her friends called to say that Brian wanted to break up with her. Then came another call from another girl who said the same thing. This time, Angie asked why. The second friend told her that Brian thought it was getting too serious.

The friend recounted the times Angie had been with her boyfriend. They reviewed the unwritten junior high school bible: the Code. The Code consists of the four sexual bases, built around the baseball game: first base, French kiss; second base, a boy feels under a girl's shirt; third base, a girl feels down a guy's pants; home base, intercourse. Angie and her friend discussed the fact that she had finally agreed to go to second base with Brian, but the next time they were together, she refused. A couple of days later was when he wanted to break up with her. Angie is so popular that she doesn't care that Brian ended their relationship. But she does care *why* he did it. Fortunately, Angie has enough hobbies going for her that she can move on easily to someone who is more respectful of her wishes.

Girls who have no hobbies or interests other than guys fall to pieces after a breakup because they can't get relief by drowning their sorrows in their fascinating activities. Until this point, nothing has been as interesting as having a guy. True to form, the Ally McBeal character is no longer the cute, ditzy young attorney she was in the beginning. Now she appears to be a nut case, desperate to get permanent lip lock. Anything short of commitment leaves her cold.

After anyone breaks up with someone they cared about, they are in pain. But the girl who has focused totally on a guy to the exclusion of everything else will be brokenhearted longer. She has nowhere to go to lick her wounds and forget. Disappointing love is why Alice feels the way she does:

Dear Dr. Gilda:

Doc, sorry to tell ya this, but I doubt I'm the first. Love sucks!!!   *Alice, 16 years old*

At 16, Alice is already aware of the pitfalls of losing your heart to someone. But how can love "suck" when being in love is meant to make us feel great?

Eighteen-year-old Christine recently told me, "I've seen my mom and dad get divorced. During her breakup, my mom said that she never wanted to be without a man. So she hooked up with a guy only six weeks after her split with my father. She's now remarried—and I don't even think she's happy. Actually, I don't see any point in ever getting married." Yet Christine admits that she wouldn't mind finding a cool guy to have a short-term relationship with. But she says that having a permanent commitment is something she never wants. She figures, "Why should I set myself up for total letdown?"

My response to Christine is that each short-term relationship is naturally followed by a probably painful split. Who needs the heartache of constant breakups? All these serial relationships can be prevented if you find someone from the start who won't disappoint you. In other words, find someone who is particularly cool for you.

My Guy Is Cool—but Is He Cool for Me?

Teenage girls are forever changing and maturing. The Centers for Disease Control has seen a falling teen birth rate of 4 percent for 15- to 19-year-olds since 1996. The total drop since 1991 has been 12 percent. Since it's the girls who give birth, those statistics tell me that you girls are becoming more responsible even though your hormones are pulling you in confusing directions. But these hormones also get you to change your minds a lot about whether a guy is right for you. (Another reason not to become young mommies.) Girls find themselves questioning whether they want to keep the boyfriend they've been seeing for a while. Or they might not know if they want to continue to date a particular guy they've been involved with, as is the case of this 17-year-old:

Dr. Gilda:
   My boyfriend is a really sweet guy, like the type that Mom and Dad have dreamed I'd bring home to them.

However, at times he is very immature. Every day I have to go through a list of questions, asking myself whether I should stay with him, or whether I should break it off. There are a lot of cons and a lot of pros. We have been together for about four months. So what should I do? Please, please help me!

Love,
A Dear Fan

Dear A Dear Fan:

No guy will ever have 100 percent of the qualities you'd like. (And by the way, princess, you'll never have 100 percent of the qualities he'd like either. Sorry!) Sometimes there will be a lot of cons, and other times there will be just a few. Complete my Make-a-Choice Quiz and I think you'll be closer to figuring it out. Let me know how it works out.   *Dr. Gilda*

Make-a-Choice Quiz

Create two lists showing the pros and cons of staying with your boyfriend. After you have written as many pros and cons as you can think of, assign a number from 1 to 5 to each item you listed, 1 being the Least Important to you, and 5 being the Most Important to you. When you're finished, add the scores you got for the pros and the scores you got for the cons. Your numbers won't lie; they'll tell you which of the two lists is more meaningful to you. Then all you have to do is act on the information that is right before your eyes.

Let's look at 15-year-old Marsha's list for her boyfriend of six months:

MAKE-A-CHOICE QUIZ

Pros

__4__ He's very affectionate when we're alone.

__4__ He goes out of his way to do little things for me.

__3__ He makes me laugh.

__4__ He treats me with respect in front of my friends.

Cons

__5__ He ignores me when he's with his friends.

__5__ Sometimes he doesn't call me for days.

__3__ He often tries to make me jealous.

__5__ He doesn't tell people that he has a girlfriend.

__2__ He rarely invites me when he goes places with his close friends.

Marsha's pros totaled 15. Her cons totaled 20. Obviously, the cons won out. From this, she learned that her boyfriend was upsetting her more than she had even realized. At first, she didn't want to accept the truth. But when we talked about it, she said out of all the cons she listed, she was especially upset after her guy would sweet-talk her with a promise to call the next day, then forgot to dial her digits. After Marsha completed this quiz, she realized how upset she really was about *all* the cons she listed.

To make the list come out better, she tried desperately to think of more pros to write, but she was stumped. As a result of this quiz, she knew it was time to take a long and careful look at whether this guy was good for her. Obviously, her heart knew the answer. Finally, as painful as it seemed, she decided to say good-bye to him and look for someone who responded to her needs in a more loving way.

The Make-a-Choice Quiz reflects what's in your heart. It tells you the truth that sometimes you don't want to face. Remember, though:

Gilda Gram	In matters of love, a girl always knows what's best for her.

Although a girl always knows what's best for her, whether she chooses to abide by the warnings is another story.

A girl who believes in herself knows that she can trust her judgment. When she is ambivalent about whether a guy is right for her, she knows she can begin to solve the puzzle by taking the Make-a-Choice Quiz. Then her heart and her head will join forces and tell her the info she needs to hear.

After a girl has decided to hear what her heart tells her, she must stick to her boundaries. A girl's commitment to her boundaries is very appealing to most cool guys. It shows them that she thinks for herself and won't be easily led. That's a challenge that cool boys enjoy. When a guy feels that his girl is independent, and is with him only because she chooses to be, he feels great about winning the heart of someone special. Let's face it: there are plenty of girls all too willing to take any guy just so they can have a boyfriend. But if your behavior projects the fact that you are choosy, and you'll only hang with a guy you consider to be terrific, your boyfriend will be pleased to have the rep of being your very special man. What's more, his friends will think that since he's won your heart, he *must* be cool. And of course, guys love it when others think they're cool.

If you're still uncertain about whether to make your man a keeper, examine A Girl's List of a Cool Guy's Traits. This list will turn your indecision into a definite verdict on the characteristics that are important to you in a guy. Of the 30 traits listed below, check out whether your current crush—or even the one you recently dumped and still are pining for— had enough of these characteristics to make you happy.

A Girl's List of a Cool Guy's Traits

1. Is he 100 percent committed to you?
2. Does he make you a priority in his life?

3. Does he aim to make you happy?

4. Is he optimistic and does he enjoy life (instead of being hostile and angry)?

5. Does he accept you as you are (or try to control you)?

6. Do you share common interests?

7. Do you share a similar sense of humor?

8. Does he communicate with you honestly and easily?

9. Does he consider your feelings (instead of saying hurtful things)?

10. Does he keep his promises—like calling when he says he will?

11. Is he self-reliant (or does he mooch off you and friends)?

12. Does he handle his disappointments well (instead of throwing temper tantrums or getting violent) when he doesn't get his way?

13. Does he tell you the truth?

14. Does he admit when he's wrong?

15. Does he include you and others in his comments (instead of selfishly talking only about himself)?

16. Is he respectful to your friends, your family, small children, and animals?

17. Does he honor you (rather than compete with you out of jealousy or possessiveness)?

18. Does he set and pursue his goals?

19. Does he pay, at least, his own way? But also, is he generous toward you?

20. Do you respect his friends?

21. Does he make his own decisions (or does he follow his friends)?

22. Does he compliment you often (instead of putting you down)?
23. Is he open to hearing your needs and feelings?
24. Does he have a strong bond with his mom?
25. Does he accept you as you are (or does he try to manipulate you with statements like, "If you love me, you'll. . . .")?
26. Does he introduce you to his friends and speak highly of you to other people?
27. Does he respect your need to work on a project, be with your friends, or veg out alone?
28. Does he show interest in an activity you love?
29. Do you admire his role models?
30. Is he comfortable with showing you affection?

This list will explain why an old relationship of yours went on the skids. It should also alert you before you take a detour down the next wrong relationship road. You deserve to be treated with respect. Clearly,

Gilda Gram   A cool guy is like a good bra: he supports you.

Are These Cool Guys? You Be the Judge

Here is a letter from a girl who had not yet taken the Make-a-Choice Quiz or read A Girl's List of a Cool Guy's Traits. Based on what you know now, would you call these guys cool—and worth keeping?

Dear Dr. Gilda:

I have a very big problem with this guy. We've seen each other for over a year, but he never asks me out. We never have a real conversation, and he never asks me anything about my life, like how is school going. He never invites me to the parties he throws, he rarely calls me on the phone, and it seems like all he wants to get from me is sex (I was so naive that I gave it to him.) He told me twice that he loved me. The first time was at the park. He was holding me tight in his arms. At the time I was cheating on my boyfriend, and I guess he wanted me only for himself. He convinced me that he loved me when he looked me in the eyes and said the three words I didn't expect him to say. I was confused because I didn't know who to choose, my then boyfriend or this guy. So I didn't say I love you back, and I guess that that made him feel uncomfortable. The second time he said "I love you" was after having sex with me for the first time. I was the one who said it first.

My problem now is that I can't stop thinking about him. I can never concentrate in school. I get so mad and jealous when he flirts with other girls that all I want to do is beat them up. I feel offended every time he makes fun of me or says bad things about me. It's just very depressing because even though he treats me like crap, I always end up falling for him bad. If he spit in my face I would still take him back. I've told myself so many times during the past year that he's no boyfriend mate-rial, and that he's no good. But it never clicks inside my head. Whenever I ignore him he always ends up com-ing back. I always think that he will eventually change, but it never happens. I'm tired of all this bullcrap but I still think that I'm in love and that these feelings will never go away, even if I try really hard. I think it's impos-sible for me to find a guy who will always respect me and love me for who I am, not for my looks. This prob-lem is affecting the people around me, as well as my per-sonal and social life. I want to be with him, but he's so unpredictable. What should I do?   *Soft Lips, age 17*

I sent Soft Lips the Make-a-Choice Quiz and A Girl's List of a Cool Guy's Traits. In addition to these, I also responded to her dilemma with this note:

Dear Soft Lips:

You certainly do have a big problem. This guy is playing you for a fool, and you know it. But I don't expect you to listen to my words any more than you have followed the advice you try to tell yourself. Instead, I'm sending you two of my assessment tools. The first one requires that you list your guy's pros and cons and then weigh them according to what you find important. This way you yourself can see what you

> really think you want in a cool guy. The second one lists
> 33 cool traits a keeper should have. After you have
> completed these assessments, please get back to me
> with your results. *Dr. Gilda*

Soft Lips must really have been hurting because she answered
my letter within only a matter of days. She said:

> *Dear Dr. Gilda:*
>
>   These were the best quizzes I could have had. The
> Make-a-Choice Quiz, especially, showed me some
> information I could not have gotten anywhere else. In
> fact, these quizzes made me come face-to-face with
> facts I didn't really want to deal with. After I wrote them
> down, I cried. These were my results:
>
> ### Pros
>
> __3__ I like calling this guy my boyfriend because he's
> very popular and it makes me feel popular, too.
> __5__ When we have sex together, I feel loved.
> __3__ I have to admit the challenge of whether he'll
> be around is exciting.
>
> ### Cons
>
> __5__ We never have a real conversation.
> __5__ He never asks me anything about my life.

___5___ The only time he calls me is to set up a date to have sex.

___5___ He's taken my mind off school and my grades are failing.

___5___ He flirts with other girls in front of me.

___4___ My problems with him have affected my relationships with other people.

___4___ I know he doesn't respect me or care about what happens to me.

Soft Lips' pros totaled 11, but her cons totaled an overwhelming 33. This got her to see in black and white how destructive her relationship with this guy was. She also saw that the pros she thought were so important to her were lightweights in comparison to the seriousness of the cons she wrote down. But Soft Lips didn't stop there. She went on to examine A Girl's List of a Cool Guy's Traits. She said that that's when her tears really came pouring out. As she went down the list, beginning with the first item—"Is he 100 percent committed to you"—she answered no, no, no, to each and every one of the 33 statements. At first she didn't believe that boyfriends could ever behave so nicely to their girls. Then, finally, one by one, she saw the truth. There are guys out there who are respectful. There are guys out there who care about the girls they're with. There are guys out there who build up the girls they're dating. Yes, she had to admit, "I have not gone after any of these guys. Maybe, as I said in my letter, I didn't think I could find a guy who will always respect me and love me for who I am . . . not for my looks." She also recognized that when she became jealous because of her roving-eyed Romeo, it was not the other girls who were at fault. So she had to abandon the idea of beating them up, because her own dude was on the make. She finally got it that the only person she had to work on was *her*. All these things provided a rude awakening for Soft Lips, and she couldn't stop thanking me.

Recently, I received a brief note from this young lady, along with her photo. Yes, she really was quite gorgeous. But standing next to her was a tall, handsome guy who looked like he adored her. In her note she said, "Finally, I found a real cool guy." Hooray for Soft Lips!

Girls should not think that there are no cool guys out there. They should recognize that cool guys do exist. These good ones don't set out to give a girl a hard time. They know who they are, they're comfortable with being themselves, they're not afraid to show their emotions, and they're happy to be loving and respectful. In fact, someone is going to be one of their girlfriends, so it might as well be you. To be the girl-friend of a cool guy, all you have to do is to know what you need. This is not so hard. You can do it by mastering the 4 Secrets of Love, which I'll show you how to do in Part II.

PART II

What Girls

Need

4 Secrets of Love

Girls Need Only 4 Secrets

Girls need to improve their guy radar for the *right* kind of guy, one who may be *sometimes* charming, yet who is not mistaken for a royal prince (or do I mean *royal pain?*) What makes a guy cool is that he's a dude who won't make a girl miserable. To find this cool boyfriend, a girl needs to know the 4 Secrets of Love:

1. Be an It Girl
2. Understand Guys

3. Create Your Own Excitement

4. Make Him a Teammate Before a Soulmate

Although no author has listed these secrets in the order in which they're written here, they are occasionally hidden in the pages of lots of books. Believe it or not, one of these is a children's book that's been around for over half a century and has been translated into different languages throughout the world. It's called *The Little Prince*, and probably the reason it's been popular for so long is that its message is not just for kids. I believe it fully explains the 4 Secrets of Love.

As the story goes, the Little Prince lives on his own tiny planet, which is inhabited by a sole flower and some caterpillars. The flower is a beautiful rose and her perfume permeates the entire planet. She's got attitude, and the Little Prince can't seem to get enough of her. Unlike any creature he has ever met (there aren't too many on his planet), this flower is not shy about asking for what she wants. The Little Prince never before heard anyone speak up for herself. She knows what she needs and she's not shy about asking for it. For example, without hesitation, she asked him to protect her from the cold and the caterpillars with a glass globe. The Little Prince did that for her.

Maybe the Little Prince felt limited by being on this tiny planet with no other men to talk to. Maybe he felt a need to hunt for adventure. Whatever his motivation, the Little Prince took off on a long expedition far away to visit asteroids and other planets. He left the flower behind to fend for herself. But she was independent enough to make it alone, especially since she had received the glass globe from the Little Prince to add to her protection.

On his journey, the Little Prince met many men. They spoke of things they thought were "matters of consequence," material things that answered the questions "How expensive?," "How much?," "How many?," "How soon?" But the Little Prince noted that these men had never seen a star, smelled a flower, or loved anyone. He knew these men were missing something *really* of consequence. Somehow he knew that the greatest things in life are not *things* at all, but feelings people share for one another.

On one of the planets he traveled to, the Little Prince came upon 5,000 flowers in one garden that all resembled the very flower on his own planet. He was amazed. Then he met a fox he wanted to befriend. The fox refused. He told the Little Prince that they could not play together until the Little Prince tamed him. When the Little Prince didn't understand the meaning of being "tamed," the fox explained that "to tame" means "to establish ties." The fox told him that after they established ties, they would need each other, they'd be committed, and they'd be unique to one another, unlike any relationship they knew with anyone else.

The Little Prince asked the fox how he could tame him. The animal said that it takes time and patience. At first, the two of them would just sit and stare into each other's eyes. Day by day they'd move closer until they felt a genuine bond. When that bond was tied, they'd know the fox was tamed.

After the fox taught the Little Prince the meaning of commitment, he told him to compare his sole flower with the garden of 5,000 he had seen. He told him that his flower would be unique to him because he had "tamed" it. It was *she* that he had watered, put under the glass globe, and protected from the cold and caterpillars. It's the *time* he had spent with her that made her special. She had become *his* rose.

With this lesson of what was really of consequence, the Little Prince returned to his tiny planet where he could be reunited with his flower. He had learned from the fox that you become responsible for and committed to whomever you have developed ties with.

I don't think it's an accident that I discovered these four secrets hidden in the pages of *The Little Prince,* while I also called the last book I wrote *Don't Bet on the Prince!* For sure, most guys have been raised to be princes of one kind or another. A lot of them believe that they are *all that* ("and a bag of chips," as my teenage niece likes to say). *All that*–type guys are conceited and cocky and think that they are better than everyone else. They manage to bamboozle a lot of the girls they meet to really believe that they are hot. Unlike the flower, these girls are reluctant to speak their mind and ask for what they need. They hold their tongues because they are afraid to rock the boat and frighten the guy off. They sit on their feelings, and guys find that the girls they originally met and liked are now boringly agreeable rather than challenging and interesting. When guys find that the girls they're with are *too* boringly agreeable, they pack them in and look elsewhere.

The Little Prince's flower was different from the girls who sit on their emotions. She was not afraid to ask for help when she needed it. And when the Little Prince decided to go on his adventure without her, she didn't plead with him to stay home. She didn't cry when he left. She accepted his desire to travel as part of who he was and what he needed to do. And she independently remained on her planet doing what she does.

Today's girls, it seems, are a far cry from the flower. For starters, many girls take the initiative and ask guys out directly. On one hand, making the first move shows a guy that you say and do exactly what you feel. Guys like girls who take the reins because it strokes their egos to have someone attentive to them. It also takes the pressure off the guy who doesn't know if a girl is interested, and is afraid of potential rejection. Although these overtures may be appreciated, there's a downside to the "get-him" approach to dating. If a guy is not interested in a girl and she pursues him anyway, she becomes an irritant that he can't wait to shake. University of Washington researchers found that 21 percent of 165 college men reported being the object of unwanted sexual attention. Some women hung around parties just waiting for guys to get drunk so that they could hit on them when their defenses were down. These girls were so anxious to get a guy to say yes that they acted desperate—the biggest turn-off of all. If the guy you're pursuing is really immature, chances are he'll want to stroke his ego further by telling his friends about your attempts. This can embarrass even the most confident.

When a guy turns a girl down, the rejection can make her feel really awful. Diane approached Derek with, "Our friends think we'd make a really good couple. How about going out?" But Derek didn't like Diane so he quickly said no. Although Diane told her friends that she really didn't care, she was obviously hurt and embarrassed. Her friend

Christie also liked Derek. Mary went up to him and asked him out for Christie. Derek at first said maybe, but he quickly changed that to yes. The whole school knows they like each other and that they're a couple. Meanwhile, Diane continues to feel bad about putting her feelings on the line and getting them smashed.

The pain of rejection can be great for girls or boys. Many girls get around it by having a friend like Mary do the asking. This way if a boy refuses the offer, the girl doesn't have to feel humiliated in front of her friends. Even so, I get loads of letters like these:

Dear Dr. Gilda,

I have a problem. I haven't had a boyfriend in over two years. There is this guy I like and he is really nice and funny. He is my best friend's cousin. She is cool with it and everything so I am not worried about that. He is two years older than me and he knows I like him (I think). I really want to ask him out but I am afraid of rejection and I would feel so awkward to go to my friend's house when he's there and have him say no. What should I do? Thanks!   *Katie, age 15*

Dear Katie,

Rejection is one of the problems you must face when you ask a guy out, or even when you ask anyone for anything. Guys face rejection all the time when they do the inviting. And they're just as fearful about being dissed by a girl as a girl is about being dissed by them.

Whenever you ask anyone for anything, they could say no. To make your life a little easier, you might want to do some serious flirting with this dude before you open your mouth with an invitation. Give him some longer, more lingering looks to let him know you're interested in something more than casual conversation. Gently brush your hand over his hand when you're giving him something. If he's got an IQ over room temperature, he's sure to pick up on the cues. What he does about them is another thing. You can continue this flirtation for a few meetings and see if he takes the hint. If he does, he'll feel it's safe enough to ask you out. If he doesn't, then you may want to bite the bullet, take the chance of rejection yourself, and do the asking. Whatever you choose, understand that if this one doesn't take the bait, there are lots of other fish in the sea. Good luck.

Dr. Gilda

Despite the possibility of being rejected, today's girls are not waiting passively for a prince as they did in the fairy tales where they went to sleep for years. They are putting the moves on guys—either on their own or through a friend. But when they do get turned down, they feel as awful afterward as Diane did. Anyone would.

To make matters worse, if the guy does agree to go out

with them, girls will tend to focus too much attention too soon on their young dudes, to the exclusion of their own needs. Their schoolwork suffers, they get into trouble with their parents, they stop enjoying the hobbies they once loved, and they often leave their friends flat. Their guys may eventually show the kind of affection the girls are after—or they may not. In the end, these girls wonder if changing their lives inside out for a guy was worth it.

Love disasters won't occur if girls realize that their needs come first. Even if they want to ask a guy out by inviting him to go somewhere special with them, they must understand that before they actually fall for him, they must first care for themselves:

Gilda Gram   The first word of "I love you" is and always will be "I."

When a girl shows a guy that she's important to herself, she also shows him how she wants him to treat her. That means that a girl should not cancel previous plans for a guy, she should not put off studying for an important test because *he* wants to hang out with her, and she should not sneak around with someone her parents hate, which will only get her grounded. When a girl sets her boundary limits, and lets her limits be known, a cool guy will have more respect for her as he understands that she's special and unique. Do you have the smarts to attract a cool guy? You will, after you follow these 4 Secrets of Love, which I call Needs.

NEED #1

Be an *It Girl*

being an *It Girl* puts the spotlight entirely on you. *It Girls* know they've got a lot going for them, and they're willing to rid the idea that their guy is everything. If you're really ready now to become *It*, you'll have to begin by recognizing that:

Gilda Gram — He's not *all that!*

Sure, he may be a terrific dude, and for the most part, he may treat you real well. But even if he has a lot going for him, be sure that you don't fall into the familiar trap where girls think their guy is so fab that he gives them the very breath they need to live. You've seen these kinds of girls—and you may be one of them, at least on occasion. They go gaga over some so-so guy, and they think they're in love. Before you know it, the girls are ready to fly to the moon to be with Mr. Wonderful. They give up doing the things that make them happy, they leave their friends flat, they ignore their parents, and they generally "drop out" of life as they used to know it. For the sake of what they call "love," they are always available, their grades suffer, and their only goal in life is to be with this guy—who, by the way, continues his own life according to his original plans. If this sounds absurd, take a look at these sad letters.

Dear Dr. Gilda:

My boyfriend is in college and I am still in high school. It seems to be working out. I just miss him and my grades are slipping because all I think about is what we are going to do the coming weekend when we will be together. Yet when we are together, we never know what to do. When we do things we have already done, we usually get bored. Please help!   *Louise*

Dear Louise:

You say this relationship seems to be "working out," but you are dead wrong. Your guy's away, pursuing his future, and you are letting your own grades and goals slip through your fingers. How is this relationship working out?? When the two of you finally do hook up, you are bored. In reality, it sounds like your relationship is in trouble. But more importantly, after the two of you part, your own poor grades will not get you into a decent college. So what will you have in the end?

Relationships are meant to support you, not drag you down. You'd better start to love yourself more than you love your boyfriend. Otherwise, you'll be without a boyfriend and without a future of your own.   *Dr. Gilda*

Guys love girls who love themselves. In case you didn't realize it, your personal Grrrl Power oozes when you know that you have what it takes to make you a popular guy-magnet. It Girls come in different shapes and sizes, and with different personalities. Some out-and-out flaunt their talent, style, looks, charm, and smarts. These girls define the difference between being *at* a party, and being the *entire* party, and because they are so extroverted, they are larger than life. But other It Girls are not so outgoing. These girls display a quiet confidence that sends the unmistakable message that they know who they are, and that they expect you to know it, too.

Just recently, within a span of two weeks, I met two very cool guys in their late 20s. Each is quite different from the other. One is a handsome white news anchor on a popular TV channel in New York. The other is a gorgeous black politician who runs a government program for inner city kids in California. Both these guys went out with the most

beautiful women in their cities. Both were confirmed bache-
lors who refused to commit to any one woman despite the
constant flow of ladies chasing them wherever they went.
But now both guys had fallen in love with someone they
intended to marry. When I asked each one what made their
special woman different from all the others they had gone
out with, each guy separately confided, "My girlfriend has a
better sense of who she is than any other woman I know."
Doesn't that tell you everything?

Somehow, a lot of females either don't feel confident
enough about who they are or only feel good about themselves if they have a boyfriend. According to Dr. Joyce
Brothers, a man falls in love at least seven times before he
finds the one he wants to spend the rest of his life with.
Unfortunately, most girls go into relationships thinking that
they are going to be "the one" that a guy will love forever.
Too many of these girls look desperate, and they pounce on
the first guy who comes along. Usually, it doesn't even matter who this guy is, as long as he is breathing. This letter is
typical of so many I receive:

Dear Dr. Gilda:

Please help. I need a boyfriend! I just can't get the
one I am crushed over! I don't know what to do! I
always try to get myself to talk to him but it just doesn't
happen! We are in a situation where it would look really
weird if I just went over and spoke to him! Please help!

Crushed in New York

Notice all those exclamation points!!! Would you rate Crushed in New York as *mildly interested* in finding a boy-friend or *gotta-hook-up-fast desperate*? I think it's clear that Crushed wants a boyfriend so badly that she'd do practically anything to get one. Don't you think a guy will pick up her desperate vibes? No guy feels good about a relationship if his girl just wants to have *any* boy rather than a *special* boy. So the first thing Crushed has to do is cool down! That will not be easy if she continues to beg for love.

Look at the names of two popular women's fragrances: Romance and Happy. Would you believe that teenage girls spent $708 million on fragrance for themselves in 1998, and an additional $420 million giving fragrance as gifts! Someone dreamed up these significant names because they represent women's emotions. Romance is supposed to make us Happy because we've been conditioned to believe that some guy who's *all that* will provide us with *all those* feelings that we believe we can't get on our own.

> *6-year-old*: "I'm in love with Fred and he loves me more than anyone else in the whole wide world."
>
> *Mother*: "Are you going to marry him?"
>
> *6-year-old*: "No, he's got hot hands."

Most girls who fall hard for a guy believe that he's more than he really is. While this 6-year-old thinks she loves Fred "more than anyone else in the whole wide world," she also realizes that she won't marry him because he has what she considers to be a fatal flaw. It's good to see that she is so picky at this early age, but notice that the flaw she has pinpointed is a superficial one. She doesn't talk about not marrying Fred because he is mean or nasty to her. When do girls begin to see the deeper, more damaging personality flaws that can affect them in a negative way? And more importantly, when does she overlook these harmful flaws and decide to connect with him *no matter what his drawbacks are* just to have someone, or really, *anyone*? Whenever that time does come and a girl accepts a guy despite the things that bother her about him, that's when she has put aside herself and her own values. As soon as a girl trashes her personal values, that's when she suffers in love.

Dear Dr. Gilda:

My boyfriend and I just got engaged. I love him to death, but we fight all the time. My mother and father have been remarried four times each. I don't want this to happen to me. I don't know if I can handle it anymore. I go to school full-time and work full-time just to get away. I don't know what I would do without him, though. I support him mentally, physically, and financially. I would do anything for him. I know he loves me a lot, but I just wish he would show it more. How do I get him to be less jealous and more lovey-dovey? I want to be able to go out with my friends without him getting mad. I want a healthy relationship with him.

How do I make it work? I know communication is the key thing. But he gets mad when I mention this stuff and we end up fighting more. *Tiffany, 18*

Dear, dear Tiffany:

If you're not happy with your boyfriend now, things will only get worse as your life becomes more complex. You are so right that communication is key to any relationship. If your guy blows up or even blows you off when you raise an issue he doesn't like, that's a warning that he can't communicate well. And it's also a pretty good indicator that this is how he'll remain.

In addition, you say you don't know what you would do without him. Yet it seems that you, yourself, are carrying the burden of the relationship by supporting him "mentally, physically, and financially." So what does he do for you, girl? If anything, he's jealous, he doesn't show you enough affection, and he allows you to do all the emotional work. To add insult to injury, you ask me how *you* can make it work. Is he not responsible for anything that goes on in your dismal duo?

You two are certainly not candidates for marriage at this time. If you intend to remain engaged, you must seek counseling before you plan a wedding. You have to sort out how you interpret your own mom and dad's marriages. Running away from your upbringing to a marriage of your own is not the solution. In fact, it will probably lead you into making the biggest mistake of your life. Please don't let that happen.   *Dr. Gilda*

When a girl feels bad in love, the problem is usually that she has put too much faith in the myth that her guy will take her to happily-ever-after land. Tiffany is trying too hard to maintain this relationship single-handedly. And how does her guy repay her? With jealousy, control, and fighting. Unfortunately, Tiffany seems to want so badly to be loved that she will automatically accept this nasty behavior from her guy, become engaged to him, and consider spending her life with him. This girl has got to wise up quickly.

Gilda Gram   Don't be so needy to have *somebody* that you end up choosing *anybody*.

Fourteen-year-old Amy is an example of that same kind of girl who is willing to settle for *anyone* just to have *someone*:

Dear Dr. Gilda:
I know I'm still young but I really need some advice on how to find that "sweet" guy I can relate to. I've been meeting guys I have nothing in common with. My

life is pretty complicated right now with a lot of problems, and I just want someone who will make me happy. Please help.

Amy

See? Amy wants Happy! Maybe this is a good choice for the name of a fragrance, but it's a bad idea for her to think that she can get Happy from either a sweet-smelling bottle or a sweet-talking guy. Amy's looking for a boyfriend who will be a Band-Aid for her "complicated problems." She doesn't yet realize that no guy can do that. Guys have their own problems, and they would love to find someone to make *them* happy, not the other way around. Girls looking for guys to rescue them should return to fairyland and sit by the cinders and wait for the handsome prince to search for their correct shoe size! When that doesn't happen, a girl had better know how to make her own happiness. Even if she's managed to find some seemingly princely guy, she'd better realize the key to happiness on her own, because this dude could always suddenly decide to leave.

Girls Who Accept "Less-Than" Treatment

Girls like Tiffany and Amy who expect their boyfriends to be *all that* often accept what I call "Less-Than" Treatment:

Gilda Gram

"Less-Than" Treatment is treatment from a guy that is *less than* okay.

Girls who fall into this category believe there's truth in the title of Britney Spears's song, "Born to Make You Happy." They are the girls whose boyfriends buy them cell phones and beepers so that the guys know their whereabouts every hour of the day. They are the girls who only feel happy about themselves when they have a boyfriend. Should the boyfriend break up with them, they immediately blame themselves. These girls put their guy on a pedestal and make him feel he can do no wrong.

Seventeen-year-old Carolyn was in a relationship—sort of—with Tony for four months. Before long, she learned that he had already had a long-term girlfriend. But he still wanted to hold on to Carolyn. For some silly reason, she decided to put up with Tony's antics for a while. She admitted, "I love him a lot. He is my life and I don't know what I would do without him." Her statement that he was *her life* was Carolyn's first mistake. It is scary to think that any girl would make a guy her life. The only person who is your life is YOU.

Carolyn bought his story, rationalizing to her friends, "He's still with this girlfriend trying to see how things are going to work out. But he lives in one state and she lives in another. They never see each other or anything so I don't think they have much of a chance together." She continued with him for another four months even though it was upsetting her that he wasn't hers completely. She refused dates with other guys, although her friends tried to talk some sense into her. But she said, "If things don't work out for him and his girlfriend, he is going to come back to me because he says he loves me. I want to share the rest of my life with him."

Carolyn's second mistake was her willingness to accept "Less-Than" Treatment by waiting around, putting her love life on hold, and accepting crumbs from a guy who couldn't decide if he wanted someone else instead of her. There's no future in accepting crumbs because:

> **Gilda Gram**   When you accept crumbs, you end up in a crummy relationship.

Now, even if Tony returns girlfriend-free, Carolyn still can't win because:

> **Gilda Gram**   What you accept, you teach.

She's *accepted* his crummy behavior for so long that she's *taught* him that it would be okay in case he ever wants to stray again. In his mind, he thinks she'd wait around indefinitely for him to decide if he wants her. If only there were seven little drawfs she could live with until he comes around, the story would sound like a page from one of our fairy tales. All she'd have to do to make this myth complete is to go to sleep—which she seems to be doing anyway as she patiently waits without any complaint. In the end, this couple could not possibly have a future.

Carolyn's third mistake, and her biggest, was that she

never believed she was somebody. If she had, she would never have agreed to put her life on hold for a boyfriend. Unfortunately, she is not alone. A lot of girls don't have enough self-confidence to believe they deserve more. This was the situation Mindy also found herself in.

Dear Dr. Gilda:

I always wanted to be somebody. If I couldn't be somebody, I'd date someone who was somebody. So I went out with a lot of popular boys at school, and then, after I graduated, I sought guys who had great jobs or who were big sports stars in my town. The problem was that these guys were so into themselves, they never seemed to care about me. I'm miserable because I can't find anyone who loves me. I want to meet someone who really cares. What should I do?   *Mindy, 18*

Mindy is a typical teenage girl who wants to find love. The problem is that she's looking to get it from guys who are bad choices. Guys who think they're *all that* often come on like King of the Hill. But deep down, they usually have low self-esteem, which they're covering up with conceited behavior. They don't feel others will think they're very special so they spend most of their time thinking only of themselves. They surely have no room left for a girlfriend. Girls who are attracted to *all that*–type guys are forever feeling let down. But, like Mindy, girls who attract guys with low self-esteem lack self-esteem themselves. The proof of Mindy's shabby self-image is found in the second sentence of her e-mail: "If I couldn't be somebody, I'd date someone who was somebody." Whether or not we'd like to admit it, we attract guys who are like us.

This is how it works. In your head, you don't believe you're special and that you could attract a cool guy. So what do you do? Your body language, voice, and words project the image that you're not valuable. You draw people to you who reinforce the negative way you feel about yourself. This makes sense because if a girl with low self-image were to attract a hotshot guy, she'd think something is wrong with him for wanting *her.*

It's amazing how other people automatically "read" your cues without having to ask you directly whether your self-image is high or low. These cues are totally designed by you. No guy can raise or lower the way you feel about yourself—unless you give him permission. If you do, that means that your inner self (your security and your confidence) is being overshadowed by your outer self (your significance and your competence). Since your inner thoughts and feelings are conveyed through your body, think positively and optimistically, because it shows. That's why the image you have of yourself will be responsible for who you attract.

In the movie *In and Out,* the main character admits he's gay right before his wedding. Predictably, his bride-to-be becomes hysterical as she reveals that her self-esteem was based on his willingness to marry her. "I thought you could make me feel like a beautiful woman instead of the girl nobody wanted," she wails. Although this movie is a comedy and the bride-to-be is a few years older than Mindy, like Mindy she felt she could only become somebody *by connecting* to a *guy.* Too many young women mistakenly feel that it is *the prince* who will awaken them from their deep (and dull) snooze and breathe life into them where they otherwise had none. The idea of expecting a guy to give *your* life meaning is a very shaky foundation for love.

At first, a guy is flattered by a girl who credits him for being *all that.* But eventually he will grow tired of carrying the burden of *her* life around with his. Guys like women who are intelligent and have a life of their own. In fact, a study of personal ads from the University of Utah found that an ad in which a woman described herself as ambitious got 50 percent more responses than ads in which women boasted of their hot looks and great bods. Ambitious women prove they have personal goals. Ambition makes a girl more interesting. If you are one of those girls who thinks that a boyfriend should live your life for you, here's a flash: most guys believe that's too much pressure, and will eventually leave a girl like you. When they do leave, where would that leave you? There are no free rides. Everyone, whether male or female, must pull their own weight. This fact shows itself especially in a relationship.

Remember those two great guys who fell in love with two women who thought highly of themselves? These guys will be forever excited and challenged by their ladies who are not shy about speaking their mind and relaying their feelings. These guys know they will not be able to pull the same nonsense they had gotten away with with their previous girlfriends. They might at first complain that their new girls are "high maintenance." But in the end, these guys will give the women they love the utmost respect. This is the most valuable gift because:

Gilda Gram   Respect is what keeps love alive.

In just a few years of dating, Mindy has learned that the guys she's been attracting are not good for her. Smart girl! Fortunately, she's a lot smarter than some of the older women I speak to who learn this lesson after many painful *decades* of dating. But now Mindy's faced with the challenge of attracting a different sort of guy. What should she do when all along she's only liked the type who caused her pain? How does she suddenly wake up worthy of attracting a worthy man? Not surprisingly, this has nothing to do with the *guys'* flaws. Instead, it has to do with Mindy herself. Clearly, she's got to change her guy radar. Instead of concentrating on having a romance with a *guy*, she must seek a romance with *herself*. At first, that may sound strange, but Mindy must learn that she can surely be somebody without a boost from a boyfriend. Why? Because:

Gilda Gram   No guy can rev your engine the way you can.

And speaking of revving your engine, what if you fell for a guy who was just as nice and sweet as could be, except for one small problem—his girlfriend? This is the story that Marla got after she had been in a relationship for four weeks:

Dear Dr. Gilda:

I am a 19-year-old female and I'm dating a 20-year-old guy. He's very sweet and he calls me nearly five times a day and visits me whenever he can. He even writes me letters and poems saying that he's starting to fall in love with me. I'm beginning to fall for him, too. The only problem we have is that he recently told me that he's kinda in another relationship. He lives with her and she picks him up from work every day. He told me that he doesn't like her, and they argue all the time. He says he wants to be with me, and he can see us getting married and all. But going out with him and being intimate is bothering me because afterwards he goes home to her bed. I really like him, and I don't know what to do.
                                                                    Marla

Dear Marla:

I love your rationalization to yourself: you say he's "kinda in another relationship," which you then go on to explain as an out-and-out living arrangement with another woman. Open your eyes! This couple is so close that she even picks him up from work. Despite what he tells you, this is no carefree romance. If you don't believe me, why not do some spying on how they behave when they're together.

There is an easy solution to your dilemma: break off all ties with this two-timer. Not only is he not emotionally available, he also wants an insurance policy that you'll be there for him *if* he leaves his girlfriend. And that's a big "if"; somehow, I bet that if you gave him the brush-off, he'd continue living where he is. The picture translates to this guy's fears about being on his own.

Please don't fall for the nonsense that he doesn't like her and that all they do is argue. Most 20-year-old guys are too immature to settle down, but this one in particular is looking for a mommy to breast-feed him. You're right to be miserable about his cheating on his girlfriend. On some level, you must also believe that since he's living with one woman and romancing another, he could easily do the same to you. Tell him to grow up and get a life. After he's away from you—and out on his own for some time—then decide if you really want to be with him. Frankly, I hope you come to your senses and realize that you deserve a real man.

Dr. Gilda

I wish Marla and all the girls like her could understand that having *no* guy is far better than being with a creep.

Unfortunately, Marla's not alone. I get thousands of letters from girls who like attached, unavailable men who continue to tell them that they're going to dump their girlfriends, stop living with them, get divorced, and any other pile of excuses. This is all hogwash.

Dear Dr. Gilda:

I started talking to my best friend's cousin and I didn't know at first that he had a girlfriend. Now I find out that not only does he have a girlfriend, but he also lives with her. I am only 17 years old, and he is 22. But I started to have very strong feelings for him. I feel kind of bad because when she goes to work, I am there in her house.

He is the person I have been looking for. He makes me feel things I have never felt before. I know I am young but I have never had these feelings before about anyone. He keeps telling me he is going to move out, but he hasn't. I have asked for advice from my friends, and they call me a home wrecker. I don't feel that I am, because this guy and his girlfriend had problems before I came into the picture. Please help!   *Chauna*

Dear Chauna:

I know it feels great to have an older guy interested in you. It also feels great to think he'd leave his girlfriend for little young you. But the reality is that this guy's a dog for leading you on while he's still living with his girlfriend. And since he's still living with her in the same house, he has some nerve to have you over there. This is outright disrespect for this girl, and for their relationship—whether he intends to remain in it or leave.

Even if this dog goes off with you, do you think you'll trust him not to do the same thing to you? Get real! Sure, you could be looked on as a home wrecker. But frankly, I'd just call you a gullible girl. Whether this couple had problems before you entered the picture is irrelevant. He also has some nerve for telling you their private business. How'd you like to *be* this girlfriend of his?

You know, what goes around comes around. Right now, you're the "other woman." One day, you could very well end up having an "other woman" interfere between you and your guy. Leave this dude. Tell yourself—and him—that you deserve more. Then go out and get it.

Dr. Gilda

Believing that you deserve the full enchilada is what being an It Girl is all about. An It Girl knows—not merely *thinks*—that she is terrific and worthy, and she projects that knowledge to each guy she meets. Look at Mindy's letter again. She says, "If I couldn't be somebody . . ." Hey, Mindy and Chauna and Carolyn and Amy, and all the girls who resemble them, there's no "if" about it: everybody *is* somebody. And you should also know that everybody who's somebody probably started out feeling like nobody—until they learned these skills. You can do it, too.

Start this minute to get your It Girl gear in motion. Lavish yourself with attention, the same kind of attention Mr. *All That* lavishes on himself. Go out and do the things you love. Buy that CD you've been longing for. Or, study passionately for that upcoming test—and set a goal of acing it! Discover that the sense of accomplishment you get is amazing. If your new ego massage doesn't feel comfortable at first, keep it going until you get used to it. Once you begin to enjoy your super treatment, you'll never understand why you hadn't begun it sooner.

When someone knows she's somebody, her positive thoughts become guy-magnets. Her love for life is contagious, and fabulous people can't stay away from her. She attracts other somebodies who are not conceited, but who are willing to give and share and love.

Gilda Gram   If you want to improve your love life, love life.

Instead of being a spectator, get out and *do*! The more exciting things you *do*, the more exciting person you *are*. When you think positive thoughts, you attract positive guys.

Gilda Gram   If you want love that won't keep letting you down, don't let yourself down.

Understand:

Gilda Gram   Feeling that you're somebody is a necessity, not a luxury.

Whether they're outwardly bold or strongly silent, It Girls think so highly of themselves, they create a buzz about themselves that others want to be around.

When I was teaching junior high school kids, I found a poster that I hung in my classroom. It said: "I know I'm somebody 'cause God don't make no junk." My students insisted on copies to take home. My smart students realized that self-pride was the key to happiness. I wonder where these students are today. I wish I knew if they remembered that lesson. Girls who *don't* think they're somebody are reluctant to stand up for themselves, and others take advantage of their sweetness. After they've been stomped on repeatedly, they end up feeling used and exhausted. It's especially painful if they've trusted their heart to a guy and have not gotten emotional support back in return.

Girls Who Don't Think They're Somebody

These girls are not alone. Plenty of girls of all ages don't think they're somebody. Unfortunately, plenty of grown women feel the same bleak way. That's why it's so important to learn the skills of somebody-building right now.

This disturbing letter from a 17-year-old high school senior who has been married for just six months is an example of a girl who needs to learn these skills:

Dear Dr Gilda:

I am very sad because my husband basically cheated on me in front of my face. See, my husband wanted to be in a multiple-person sexual situation, which I agreed to. We did this with my best friend and his wife. My best friend and I were way too close to even think of touching each other and so we just stopped and looked at each other and laughed. However, my husband continued going with his wife. My best friend and I even walked out of the room and they still kept going. My husband does not understand why I am upset. Do I have a right to be upset? Please help me.

June

What disturbs me most as an educator and therapist is the next-to-last sentence: "Do I have a right to be upset?" Only a girl who doesn't think she's somebody would ask that question. Girls who don't think they're somebody believe they have no right to their emotions. These girls are too self-conscious to express how they feel. They often rush to get married as a way to escape from their life. This doesn't work. Look at Drew Barrymore, married to a bar owner at 19, and divorced a mere two months later. Look at Milla Jovovich, married to an actor at 17, and divorced after her mom had it annulled, then married again at 22 to a director, and divorced at 24. Look at Jennie Garth, married to a musician at 22 and divorced two years later, just seven months before giving birth to another guy's baby. Girls who have not yet had enough experience living should not be committing themselves to lifelong ties. Now look at June, barely out of high school yet married, questioning whether she has the right to feel. This is so pitiful because:

Gilda Gram   Our feelings are a wonderful part of what makes us special.

Girls Who Know They're Somebody

A study at Lafayette College found that very smart students are often teased for being gifted. While boys often fend off negative reactions by becoming the class clown, girls simply deny their intelligence altogether. While in the short term, "dumbing down" allows them to fit in, these girls are learning to limit their potential and lie about who they really are. People who live a lie about being someone they're not learn to bury their wit, feelings, and social skills.

No matter who she is, every girl has not only a right to her feelings, but an obligation to express them. Girls who express that they're somebody are the *It Girls*. It Girls don't believe they're *all that*. *All that* types are conceited and cocky. It Girls know they're popular, understand they're smart and are not afraid to show it, feel they're cool, and love life. When it comes to guys, they would rather not be with *just anyone* for the *wrong* reasons. Instead, they'd rather be *alone* for the *right* ones. It Girls also demand to be heard. They will confront people who try to take advantage of them. In fact, just the way they carry themselves sends the message, "You want me to do what? I don't think so." So usually, these girls are not even approached to put themselves on the line and compromise their values. Simply, guys know that these girls will never accept being their doormats. It Girls often just have to look at someone and that person knows not to mess with them.

How to Become an It Girl

What gives an It Girl her "Itness"? The answer is simple: confidence. Confidence is the faith you have in yourself that lets you and everyone around you know that you have unshakable self-respect. To respect someone is to accept her. An It Girl's self-respect shows she likes herself and that she feels secure about the person she is.

Feeling Secure Versus Feeling Significant

Secure girls feel happy about *who they are*, as opposed to *what they do*. This means that no matter what stupid mistakes they make each day, they're still glad to be who they are. It also means that secure girls will not always compare themselves to others to make them feel below par. The It Girl's *security* comes from inside. Feeling secure protects her even when she has those negative feelings and occasional bouts of self-doubt that everyone experiences from time to time. Because it's inside her, her security is guarded by her whole body. No one else has the power to shatter it. This letter is from an It Girl who feels secure about who she is despite her questions of what she should do about her boyfriend:

Dear Dr. Gilda:

During my first year in high school, I met this cute guy. I became curious about him and decided to become his friend. It turned out that he is one of the friendliest, sweetest, and most charming people I know. We have become incredibly good friends. We talk about anything, anytime. I have realized that my initial infatuation has now turned to real caring and warm feelings. After graduation, I went to college and now we are 500 miles apart. We still keep in touch and on my occasional trips to his area, we always go out. When he has a chance, he comes to visit me, too. Should I risk this beautiful friendship by disclosing that I care for him more than as a friend? Should I wait?   *Carrie, 19 years old*

Dear Carrie:

I receive a lot of questions like yours about when and how to act on a friendship that is developing into love. The difference between your question and the others I get is that you and your guy have spent at least four years getting to know each other. You have doubts about whether he romantically cares for you, and I'm sure he has an issue about whether you feel the same for him. So now your question is more about timing than about whether you stand a chance. I'd recommend that whenever you feel most comfortable, gently ask him where he thinks your relationship is going. Let him talk freely. What he says—and even doesn't say—and the way he looks at you and touches you when he says it will let you know what's really going on in his heart. I would say that, from the sound of your letter, there's a lot happening between you, and it just hasn't yet been stated. You be the judge. When you think the time is appropriate, raise the question. I believe you'll be pleasantly surprised. Please let me know.   *Dr. Gilda*

When a girl is *secure*, she doesn't feel at risk about asking a guy what's up with their relationship. She knows that even if he says "nothing," of course she'll be hurt and disappointed, but she'll be able to go on and continue to feel good about herself even if it means being without him.

Test your own feelings of security. You are wearing a new outfit. No one has complimented you on it all day. How do you react? Do you feel depressed or upset that no one noticed? If so, this suggests that you are uncertain about your own feelings of worth, and that you're in need of an outside source to justify your taste. Girls who feel secure *know* they're cool and that they're It!

In contrast to feelings of security, which have nothing to do with where you are or the people who surround you, feelings of *significance* depend not on your confidence, but on how *competent* you feel with the externals around you. In other words, significant feelings consist of what you achieve, which friends you have, and how situations affect you. Obviously, these are changeable situations, so, unlike your security, your significance can alter.

Apply the same test of security we just discussed above. If no one complimented that great new outfit you were wearing, you would feel *insignificant*, even though you still might feel secure about who you are as a person. Significance pinpoints your self-esteem because to esteem is to evaluate. The problem with evaluation is that sometimes we're evaluated positively, and sometimes we're not. The good thing about the changing feelings of significance is that once a girl removes herself from negative surroundings, she can watch her competence—and significance—soar.

I recently received this letter from Sari, a 16-year-old girl in conflict. Do you think that Sari is feeling insecure or insignificant?

Dear Dr. Gilda:
   I have a problem with my boyfriend. I can't trust him anymore. The reason why is that he has been selling

porn magazines on his bus and at school. He said he got rid of them for me, but a little while later I saw him selling some more. The only time we talk is on the phone once or twice every two weeks. He doesn't look at me anymore and I think it is because he'd rather look at some naked women he doesn't know. My question is should I dump him?

Sari, age 16

Dear Sari:

You already know what to do. This guy makes you feel bad by not paying attention to someone he calls his girlfriend. Also, he's doing things you don't respect. Dump him now and attract someone new who looks forward to being with you and is into activities that you feel good sharing with him. While your so-called "boyfriend" drools over the make-believe images in the magazines, you'll have a *real* guy who gives you what you need.

Dr. Gilda

Sari doesn't feel significant around her boyfriend, but she feels secure enough to understand that there is a problem that she wants to solve. Dumping this dude is her way out of her insignificant feelings, although she's obviously not looking forward to taking that step. But she knows in her heart what she wants to do. Her letter is just asking me to give her the reassurance that she's doing the right thing.

Because they're dependent on other people and situations, feelings of significance can alter in a moment's time. For example, if you get a good grade in biology, you feel significant, but if you get into a screaming match with your best friend the next day, you may not feel significant at all. You may still be basically secure about who you are as a person, but the latest situation in your life has bummed you out, making your feelings of significance wobbly.

So while you must develop an unchanging sense of *internal* confidence, *external* confidence can alter depending on the situation. That's okay as long as you still feel good about yourself deep down so you'll move away from the negative people or situations. The feelings of internal confidence will allow you to handle any external situations in the best possible way.

When Does Being an *It* Turn to Being a (Sh)it?

There's a difference between being confident and being cocky. Make the distinction yourself after you read the next scenario. I was a guest on one of the daytime talk shows about teens who dress too sexy. When the curtain opened to introduce Deanna, 15, out walked a chubby girl in a tiny skirt and tank top. As she strutted past the other guests on the panel, she crowed, "I am the bomb." The audience catcalled at her. When she sat down, someone criticized her with this comment: "You may be able to squeeze into that little outfit, but it doesn't mean it's your size." She shot back with, "I love showing off my body. I have a great butt, chest, and face. I can get any man I want. Anyone who has a problem with me is just jealous." The audience booed.

Would you call Deanna confident or cocky? While I was doing a keynote speech for several hundred high school students, I asked this question: "What's the difference between being confident and cocky?" A thin young woman responded, "When you're cocky you have to tell everyone how great you are. When you're confident, all you have to do is show up; everyone will know you're great." Ohhh, was this girl brilliant!

For sure, Deanna's cocky attitude turned people off. I explained on the show that confident people walk into a room with the attitude, "Here I am, world . . . now tell me about you." Cocky people walk into a room with the attitude, "Here I am, world . . . and who cares about you?" Cockiness is often a cover-up for feeling crappy about yourself, and it's certainly the quality in guys you want to avoid. On the other hand, being confident is inviting. You feel good enough about yourself to invite others to share your feelings. You are anxious to give to others, and because of your caring attitude, others want to be around you.

Think about Deanna again. Did she really think she was "the bomb"? Forgetting about her trashy clothes for a moment, would you define her as someone who has a caring attitude? As we got further into how she feels about herself *beneath* her clothes, we saw a scared, insecure girl who was looking to attract attention from guys. She never realized that:

Gilda Gram   Attracting *attention* is not the same as attracting love.

Deanna thought that by wearing revealing clothes, she'd get someone to love her. When she understood the poor quality of the guys she was luring, she reconsidered. She came away from the show feeling that she did not have to flaunt her body to be appealing. After the show, she told me that she learned that:

| Gilda Gram | Less is more. |

That was a big lesson for this young lady. Not only didn't she have to get practically naked to be a guy-magnet, neither did she have to remind people in words how terrific she was. I think she finally understood that confidence, not cockiness, is where it's at. And when she really had it, everyone would know.

As the saying goes, "talk is cheap." Do you believe the talk that Leah is offering?

Dear Dr. Gilda:

I really don't know what my boyfriend thinks about me. Well, I think he might not have the right impression of me. He might think of me as an innocent home girl. Well, I'm not. How can I prove to him what I am? How can I let him know that I am *all that*?   Leah

Dear Leah:

You may want to be *somebody*, you may want to be an *It Girl*, but you don't want to act like you're *all that* because that phrase takes on the negative connotation of being conceited and cocky. Instead, become an It Girl. When you do, your boyfriend will know it, your friends will know it, and every other person you know will know it.

To tell whether you've got It traits, start examining your body language, voice, and words. Are they making the impression you'd like them to make? To check, ask your nearest and dearest friends to level with you about how you're coming across. If it turns out that you are projecting an *all that* attitude, change it to becoming an It Girl. Then, if your so-called boyfriend doesn't get how fine you are, he may be too dense for you. But what you don't want to do is have to knock him over the head by telling him so that he becomes intimidated by your strength.

When you're an It Girl, your qualities come from within. But once you feel you have to *discuss* who you are, that shows you're not confident. Become confident and the real you will shine.   *Dr. Gilda*

Despite what they say, girls who have to actually say they're somebody really don't feel great about themselves. When you're somebody, you are comfortable about just being real. You don't have to tell a soul. Everyone already knows.

How Confident Are You?

How do you measure your confidence? You've heard about IQ, or Intelligence Quotient, the score used to gauge how smart you are. Well, I've developed a score for CQ, or Confidence Quotient, a measurement to tell you if you really *believe* that you're somebody. It Girls have a high CQ. Since your aim is to strengthen your own internal confidence, the questions on this quiz relate to the *security* of who you *are* rather than to the *significance* of what you *do*. With this quiz, like all the others in this book, there are no right or wrong answers. Your scores will simply give you an idea of how you feel about yourself now. Take the CQ Quiz and check out whether you are ready to become an It Girl.

WHAT'S MY CQ (CONFIDENCE QUOTIENT)? QUIZ

Mark a "T" (true) or "F" (false) after each statement:

1. I often blame my parents for the way my life is.

2. When I attract popular guys it's not because of my charm, but because of my luck.

3. I often think, "I wish I were prettier."

4. I consider myself unattractive if I don't have at least one guy interested in me all the time.

5. When a guy begins to like me, I usually think it won't last.

6. I place a lot of value on what other people think of me.

7. I'm not usually comfortable telling guys how I really feel.

8. When I meet a new guy, I often think, "Why bother; he won't like me anyway."

9. I usually feel uncomfortable when people compliment me or give me gifts.

10. I rarely set goals for myself.

11. I prefer to belong to a popular crowd.

12. When I lose at something, I feel bad about myself.

13. I don't especially like myself a lot of the time.

14. When my friends criticize me, I feel dissed and dismissed.

15. I often feel bad because others are prettier, have more money, or are more popular than I am.

16. I don't make friends easily.

17. I don't want to hurt others' feelings by disagreeing with them.

18. I don't enjoy being alone.

19. I feel uncomfortable talking freely to others.

20. The thought of being bold is somewhat frightening.

Score Card

A high Confidence Quotient means you believe in yourself. If you had 3 or more Trues, your CQ needs an uplift. When you believe in yourself, others will believe in you, too, especially the terrific guys you want to attract.

Frieda is another girl who needs some confidence boosting:

Dear Dr. Gilda:

Hi! I am 15 years old. On Halloween, my friend Jenny had a party and we were gonna go trick-or-treating together. She invited me and four other friends. We decided to dress in black and put dark makeup on. We were having a blast. Jenny's cousin, Dallas, was over. He's 17. He was playing PlayStation and we were about ready to leave. When we got back, he was still there and we ordered pizza and watched movies. Then he left and the rest of us stayed the night at Jenny's.

My problem is that since that night, I have had a major crush on Dallas. I think about him a lot and Jenny tells me that he knows I like him. I'm not absolutely sure about that. She says that she wants to talk to him and see if he will go out with me. I don't have very much confidence in myself. I am overweight. I weigh 180 pounds, but my friends tell me I don't look THAT bad. I am totally afraid that he won't like me and that if I ever go to Jenny's again and he's there, I will feel uncomfortable.

Dallas and I get along pretty well. We talk sometimes when I'm there and I know him pretty well. Do you have any advice to give me on this? If my friend talks to him, what should she say? Is there anything I can do to maybe get him to like me more? What if he thinks I am too fat? Help!   *Frieda*

Dear Frieda:

I've never liked the idea of one girl doing the talking for another. One of my teenage consultants, my niece Erin, tells me that in her school, having someone speak to a guy for you is common in seventh grade. But by the time a girl gets to the ninth grade, it's up to her to hook up herself. Of course, these customs differ depending on what community you live in.

It's not Jenny's business to get you and Dallas together. If he's interested in you as a girlfriend, he'll give you the signs. But more important than whether Dallas likes you, or whether he thinks you're too fat—or too thin—is the question of how you feel about yourself. Actually, Dallas's existence in your life is showing you that you have a big problem with self-confidence, by your own admission. So what you must work on now is not getting Jenny to get Dallas to give you an answer. It's for you to do some major work on yourself.

Study the information that follows. Learn the traits of an It Girl, take the CQ Quiz, and review the ways to boost your Confidence Quotient. Many girls who believe they're special find that their extra pounds just melt right off them. Whether or not that's the case for you, once you boost your self-confidence, you may be in a position of deciding whether *you* want *Dallas*, not the other way around!

Often, the issue we *think* we need to address is not really the issue we *need* to address. Your issue is your self-confidence, not your interest in this guy. Bump up the way you feel about yourself and see how your whole life improves.   *Dr. Gilda*

How Do I Raise My CQ?

Okay, after taking the last quiz, you discovered that your CQ needs a jolt. To raise it, follow these three simple steps: Believe, Conceive, Achieve.

Step #1: Believe
Believing in yourself first requires that you recognize the payoffs of a high level of confidence. High CQ will attract boyfriends and girlfriends who are as confident as you. Notice that the It Girls in your school hang out with other It Girls. It goes with the Gilda-Gram that says, "We attract people who are like us." Confident people feel good about

themselves, and because they do, they are able to feel good about others without feeling jealous or envious. When people feel good about each other, they develop ties and become committed, the way the Little Prince became committed to the fox. Take a moment to visualize yourself at a party. Not at all nervous, you are dressed to impress. Imagine yourself entering the room as if you own it. Be friendly and strong. Stand tall and act perfectly in charge. Accept compliments gracefully. As soon as you believe in yourself, others will believe in you, too.

Step #2: Conceive

The next step to raising your CQ is to conceive a plan to make it happen. Feeling confident doesn't just occur on its own. You must be determined to work at it. You must vow that you'll avoid self-limiting statements like "I can't do that" or "He'll never like me."

Elizabeth wanted Craig to like her. They went out a couple of times and he tried to feel her breasts. She said that she wasn't ready to do "sex things" with him yet, but all her friends were already doing them, so she admitted to feeling pressure to conform. But she also didn't want Craig to lose interest in her, so she was torn about how to handle the situation. If she had had a high CQ, she would have been able to tell herself that it would be *she*—not Craig—who would decide when *she* was fully ready. Instead, Elizabeth ended up telling herself, "I can't say NO to him. He'll dump me for some other girl who will let him do these things." She continued to be his girlfriend and gave in to doing "sex things" with him even though she didn't feel ready for them.

If you, like Elizabeth, have ever been torn between what's right for you and what's not, give yourself a boost in the confidence department. Write "I can't say NO" on a piece of toilet paper and then flush it down the john. Get my drift? Now, whenever you feel down and out, write another self-limiting expression on more toilet paper, and flush that away as well. Get in the habit of flushing away all the negative thoughts that keep you from making powerful decisions that will attract the right people into your life. Then agree to sign the 10-Step CQ Booster contract:

10-STEP CQ BOOSTER CONTRACT

1. I will give myself a full hour of pure pleasure—anything that makes me feel great.

2. I will buy that new CD I've been dying to get, and I'll play it a gazillion times.

3. In my journal, I'll write two positive things each day no matter how awful the day was.

4. I'll stand naked in the mirror and say three admiring things about my beautiful image.

5. This week I'll return to my favorite hobby that I haven't enjoyed in a long time.

6. I will round up my fan club of friends for at least two hours of fun and laughter.

7. I vow to do something BOLD each day.

8. I will do a good deed, like volunteering in a hospital, working in a soup kitchen, or collecting money for a charity.

9. I will dump the so-called "friends" who drain me.

10. I will choose a role model who shows confidence. I'll study her and try to learn her secrets.

This is a promise I agree to keep with myself.

Signed: _____

When you have a high CQ, you begin to exercise your voice about what is right for you. Sometimes you have to raise that voice because a person who wants you to do something else is trying to change your mind.

Dear Dr. Gilda:

I have a big problem. My boyfriend wants to have sex with me. He thinks sex would be a way for him to hold on to me and for us to be closer. He believes this strongly because his friends have done it and they say it's great. He wants to be like them. I already told him no and he knows I'm not backing out. I truly believe he loves me and he's not using me. Besides, he respects my decision and he says it's not physical love that we have. But I want to show him there are other ways. I want him to think differently about me. He talks about having sex as if this was a life-or-death situation . . . and that scares me!

I want to find other ways for us to feel closer as a couple. Besides, we are very young and not ready for sex. I've told him how I feel but his father told him that having sex together was the best way for him to hold on to me. He said that a counselor at his school said the same thing. I want him to know I'm not going anywhere, so he doesn't have to hold on to me like that!!

Please help me as quickly as you can. I know you're busy.

Fifie, 16

Dear Fifie:

Good for you for knowing how you feel and sticking to your guns. Any guy who really loves you will respect your wishes without pressuring you to give in to his. I find it hard to believe that this guy's father and a school counselor told him that sex was the way he should hold on to you. Where would these adults be if you became pregnant, or if you contracted a sexually transmitted disease? It's only YOU who would be left to worry about this in the end. You even admit that you're both not ready to take on such a commitment.

Although you admit that you're not emotionally ready for sex, you're certainly mature enough to speak your mind. You are to be applauded. This guy may love you in his own way, but it seems like a very selfish way of loving. Is this how you'd like to spend the next years of your life—with a guy who's interested only in satisfying his own desires? I think he's not being fair to you or caring about your needs.

If your boyfriend doesn't stop pressuring you, you'd better find another guy who hears what you're saying. You deserve to be heard and cherished, not pressured.

Dr. Gilda

A girl who knows what is right for her, no matter what anyone else says, is on her way to achieving good things in life. That's a girl with a high CQ.

Step #3: Achieve

Signing the above contract will put you on the road to achieving a stronger CQ. Remember how amazed the Little Prince was to see 5,000 roses that all looked like the rose he knew on his own tiny planet? Remember how he had to learn that his rose was different from the others? As you begin to raise your CQ, you must fully understand that you are unique from all the different people around you. Your differences are what make you special. Take the next quiz and find out what your special and unique qualities actually are.

What Makes Me Special and Unique? Quiz

1. The most positive messages my parents gave me were:

2. Three cool words that describe me are:

a. _____

b. _____

c. _____

3. My greatest accomplishment is:
4. My best friend would say my best trait is:
5. In school, I'm most proud of:

Score Card

Ask friends to take this quiz, too. Compare your answers and see how theirs differ from yours. Notice that you're all special and unique in your own way. Actually, if we were all the same, life would be pretty boring. Study your special qualities. These are the traits you should be proud of.

Remind yourself often:

Gilda Gram

I am special and unique.

Unlike the toilet paper you flushed down the john, this Gilda Gram should be written on your mirror and on stick-'ems around your room so you can see them everywhere you go. Always think of your own magnificence.

Gilda Gram   To raise your CQ, believe, conceive, achieve.

Are you convinced of your own uniqueness yet? Let's narrow your special qualities down to specific traits. On the next quiz, circle the words that you believe describe you. Then give the list to a good friend and have him or her circle the words that she or he feels apply to you. Compare the two lists to see how similar or different they are.

POSITIVE PERSONALITY TRAITS QUIZ

active	considerate	gentle
affectionate	creative	genuine
ambitious	dependable	good-natured
assertive	determined	helpful
attractive	entertaining	humorous
caring	enthusiastic	happy
cheerful	friendly	independent

intelligent	self-confident	trusting
likable	sensitive	truthful
organized	serious	warm
outgoing	sincere	Other Traits:
patient	sympathetic	

Score Card

This quiz is like looking in a mirror. It is a good way to check out your own personality traits as you see them, and also to test how you appear to a friend. Besides those that you and your friend circled, were there other traits you thought should be included? If so, add them to your list, get feedback from your friends about those you've added, and begin to think of them often.

Acting Out Your Traits

Each day, select a favorite circled word from your list. Look at yourself in the mirror, and strike a pose that expresses that word. For example, if you chose "entertaining," pose, walk, and look like an *entertaining* person. Enjoy each trait—as only you can. Then go to school with your trait in mind. Without telling anyone what you're doing, except maybe your best friend, act out that word all day. Keep a log of people's reactions. Remember that these are all positive words, so you can't ever fail. You'll just be exploring different parts of your personality that you had never thought of before. Remember, love life, and above all, have fun!

A Word of Caution

You're on your way to achieving your plan for a higher CQ. But there is one thing you need to keep in mind as you start to make changes. When you're becoming an It Girl, others will surely notice. The so-called "friends" who knew you when your CQ was lower will sense something different about you. They probably won't know what to make of the new you because girls with a high CQ attract lots of attention from guys. Not that that's your goal. But being an It Girl is so wonderful that *everyone* notices. But just because they notice, don't expect everyone to be happy for you. In fact, don't be surprised if some of your friends now say that you think that *you're all that*! Of course you know better. You know that raising your CQ is not a selfish or conceited act at all, but rather, a gift you are giving yourself to make you feel better. And the added bonus is that you'll attract more *worthy* guys. But your friends will probably try to get you to change back to the original you that *they* were comfortable with. (Check out who's really being selfish here!) To make yourself feel better and to give you an added boost, remember that your friends' judgments are not your problem.

Gilda Gram   You are only responsible for yourself and your own actions.

What will probably happen is that you'll enjoy your new self-confidence and the new kind of attention you're getting from guys—and girls—you weren't attracting before. You'll probably also get tired of your friends' badgering. You'll want to develop friendships with people who are more supportive. Keep in mind that moving on to new friendships is a positive thing. It will be your friends' loss, not yours, as you meet new people who will give you the kind of caring to which you're entitled.

Outshouting Your Inner Critic

Despite all the work you've done to convince yourself you're terrific, sometimes parents, friends, siblings, or teachers can unknowingly say something negative to you that you can't get out of your mind. Some of these put-downs actually become what I call your negative "voice," or your self-doubting inner critic. Sometimes, this voice could shout so loudly that it overpowers the one with a high CQ. Imagine what happens if your CQ is still a little shaky while it's in the process of getting stronger. Your critical voice might trigger a short episode of self-bashing. Self-bashing often occurs when you least want it to, like when that cute guy finally approaches you and asks you out. If you allow your inner critic to get the better of you, you might find yourself tongue-tied and unable to project your most positive vibes. You may start saying stupid things or sounding like a jerk. If that's your situation, stop right there. Instead of allowing your inner critic to control you, follow the 4-Step Plan to Silence Your Inner Critic:

4-Step Plan to Silence Your Inner Critic

1. Acknowledge what your inner critic is trying to do, and be ready to talk back to it.
2. Write down or say out loud each negative thought your inner critic is sending your way.
3. Immediately write positive substitute thoughts beside the negative ones.
4. Convert each negative thought into a new goal.

Alice desperately wanted John to notice her. Finally, he was walking her way. "Omigod," she thought. "What will I do?" She began to feel her inner critic taking charge and she knew that was not a good thing. So this is what she did:

1. *Alice's Inner Critic:* "Uh-oh. Here comes John. Oh, no! I am sooo fat."

2. *Alice Said Out Loud,* "I am sooo fat."

3. *Alice's Positive Statement:* "No, I am NOT sooo fat; I just *feel* fat. I'm still the same clothes size I was yesterday. But I am 4 pounds over my usual weight and I want to lose these pounds. That should take only two weeks."

4. *Alice's Goal:* "Starting today, I'm cutting out the rich desserts I've been enjoying. I can deal with that later. Right now I'm gonna make an impression on John."

Improving Your Confidence When You're Blue

It would be great to think that It Girls feel good about themselves all the time. But we know better. Everyone, without exception, has down days. Like other girls, It Girls get zits, they occasionally feel fat (especially during their periods), and they sometimes argue with their best friends. But unlike other girls, It Girls have enough internal security to make a bad situation a better one. They'll apply their favorite face cream to their zits and laugh that the zits will eventually disappear when they are ready, not before. They'll wear baggy clothes on down-and-out days and they won't make a big deal out of feeling puffy. They'll make the first move toward patching things up with their best friend without feeling that they've lost face.

Girls with good internal confidence can handle the down time better than those who don't think well of themselves. Why? Because people with strong feelings of security remember that they are worthy of good things, and they know that momentary lows are a fact of life that will eventually pass. In addition, girls with a strong sense of security know what to do to change a bad situation. This is why internal confidence matters more than external confidence (feeling significant). Girls with internal confidence can make bad situations improve more quickly. They can take lemons and make lemonade. It Girls are secure girls. They know they've got girl power and they take charge. With a high CQ, they're willing to be in control of themselves without trying to control others. This sense of confidence is especially important when it comes to guys. Guys enjoy hunting for adventure. Because It Girls enjoy who they are even when guys are not around, they do their own thing and have fun with their hobbies and friends. If and when the guys return, they are that much stronger to deal with them on their own terms, especially once they understand them, which I will explain next.

NEED #2

Understand Guys

There is no question that girls have better relationships with guys once they understand how they think and function. Guys and girls are quite different, with different bodies, different hormones, and different brain structures—all of which determine differences in behavior. This is not to say that one gender is better than the other. It's just that they are *different*.

For almost ten years, a battle has been brewing over which sex is most discriminated against by our schools. A 1992 study by the American Association of University Women reported that schools shortchange girls by holding them back in science subjects, and by not recognizing their opinions in class, thereby damaging their self-esteem. But since the Columbine murders, boys have been identified as the ones with the problems. Studies show that girls get better grades, are more verbal, and are more likely to attend college, while boys demonstrate poor reading and writing skills. The recent rash of high school killings has uncovered a well-camouflaged low self-esteem among boys. Since most boys are considered to be hyperactive, especially compared with girls, the school structure and demand for obedience create frustrated and aggressive young men. Whether or not schools favor one sex over the other, the differences between males and females is becoming more apparent. There are 10 million male teenagers in America. Any girl who wants to succeed with just one of them had better understand where he's coming from.

For starters, just as a car needs gas to run, guys are juiced by testosterone. Human males produce 7 to 10 times more testosterone than females. Testosterone pushes guys to grow taller, develop muscles, be more aggressive, compete, and want sex. Joshua at Teenwire.com says, "Guys talk about getting laid as often as possible. As guys, we're supposed to be gettin' it whenever and wherever we can. The talk is completely different for girls—only 'sluts' give it up . . ." In contrast to guys' testosterone, girls have a supply of estrogen and progesterone, which cause a girl to develop into a woman, get pregnant, give birth, and bond with her baby as well as her man. Because girls menstruate, we are more aware of the mood swings and changes that females naturally experience. Periods and PMS act as a sort of monthly reminder of the changes our bodies are experiencing. Since boys don't have those same triggers, girls sometimes don't realize that they are going through many body changes, too. Hormones often flood the bodies of teens more quickly than their minds can handle. These are substances in certain parts of the body that enter the bloodstream and often influence behavior. The rush of some hormones can cause teens to feel like fully grown adults at times, yet just a few moments later, they can switch back to feeling like kids. Not only can these changes be frightening when they occur, they can also be confusing. The rapidly fluctuating mood swings can cause teenagers to feel like strangers even to themselves.

Hormonal changes can't be predicted from moment to moment and even your body is confused as it's in the midst of maturing. Remember when you first got your period? Remember how irregular it was, with some skipped months, months with heavy bleeding, and some months that were so light you hardly noticed you had it? Some girls take years before they become "regular," and some never have regularly predictable periods. Although guys don't bleed, they have hormonal swings just like you, and their emotions can see-saw from one extreme to another.

After knowing Ray for a few years as a friend, Joanie figured out that he was guilty of flip-flopping his emotions when they began to date. With a lot of frustration, she said, "He's on my volleyball team, which at first I thought was pretty cool. But now he's ruining it for me. He yells at people when they miss a pass, and he's really rude to everyone in the game. That's what happens during first period. Then during ninth period when we have biology together, he's a totally different person. He's a Jekyll and Hyde personality: an asshole in gym, then a Romeo when we're in class together.

Guys transform into complete and utter idiots when they're involved in sports. I've noticed that there's not one guy I know who's normal when he's playing sports. They get into an ego trip, and you see a totally different side of them. Then you say, 'Wait, I liked *him*?' But then, out of the blue, he does something so sweet, and you think that you're the crazy one!"

Joanie's right. Ray and his friends are, indeed, Jekyll and Hyde characters whose interests and moods change at the drop of a hat. In fact, this fickleness is so much a part of being a teenage boy, that the Paramount Network (formerly UPN), a television network that boasts a large young male viewership, plans to capitalize on boys' limited attention spans by developing a number of 15-minute shows for its audience, rather than the usual 30- to 60-minute programs. The feeling is that since this is what boys this age need, the network wants to give them what they appreciate. But for most girls, boys' unpredictable changes are just plain weird.

Dear Dr. Gilda:

I need help. My boyfriend (who I really love) sometimes acts a little weird. One day he says he loves me and the next day I try to sit by him and he yells at my friend and tells her to make me sit somewhere else. I don't understand him! Now his friends have been telling me things about him liking someone else. I'm being driven crazy. Please help!!   *Karen, 14*

There's a reason for a boy's flip-flop behaviors. Guys typically get five to seven surges of testosterone a day, with an average of eleven erections. Five of those eleven occur while they're sleeping. These testosterone surges stimulate a boy's desire to masturbate a lot, and to think about sex. The testosterone surges also make these guys think they're Rambo. They act aggressively in sports, have fights, do dangerous things, act competitively in school or at their jobs, or just plain show off.

It may seem like girls are the only ones concerned about their body and their looks. But that's not so. Boys, too, worry about their image and shape. The muscular male action figures of dolls like G.I. Joe are promoting the same unrealistic expectations in guys that girls have suffered from for years. Along with the eating disorders they now share with girls, guys also crave huge biceps and an extreme desire for competition and control.

Anyone would think the testosterone urges are driven by the sex glands. But actually, their source is the three-pound blob of gray and white matter known as the brain. Researchers who once believed that brain development was complete by puberty have now found that teenage brains are works in progress. In teens, the part of the brain to control emotions and make good judgments is not yet formed. And boys have an additional part of the brain that swells as a result of their surging hormones, which may intensify aggression.

Brains are divided into the left and right hemispheres joined by a cluster of nerves called the corpus callosum. The left side of the brain controls analytical thought and precise language—at which many boys excel. The right side of the brain is responsible for creativity and intuition, which many girls display. Although this is not the case for *all* males and females, these patterns form generalizations from which we can learn.

Boys' brains are about 10 percent larger than girls' brains, but the corpus callosum is thicker in the brains of girls, making it easier for them to quickly switch back and forth between left-brain and right-brain activities. In other words, the thick corpus callosum of girls allows them to brainstorm about relationships on the phone with friends (a right-brain function), and, *at the same time*, solve complex math homework problems (a left-brain function). In contrast, because of their thin corpus callosum, guys find it easier to perform activities on one side of the brain at a time, completing one undertaking before tackling another. Because of the way their brains are wired, girls use more vocabulary words than boys, they speak more freely about feelings, and they use more variety in their language. So if a guy makes a girl angry, she may cut him down with her words (and probably leave him dumbfounded since he doesn't have such a fine ability with words to retaliate). In contrast, when a guy becomes angry, he's more prepared to react in a loud and violent way.

As the world recently witnessed the violence at Columbine High School in Colorado, reports began comparing that incident to similar shootings in schools around the country. The geographic locations have been widespread: Arkansas, Oregon, Georgia, Washington, Mississippi, and Kentucky, to name just a few. It's no accident that these violent acts were all committed by boys. Michael Gurian, author of *The Good Son,* and Kathleen Parker of *USA Today* offer these disturbing facts:

- *Emotionally disturbed boys outnumber girls 4 to 1.*
- *Boys are 4 times more likely to commit suicide.*
- *Boys are 4 times more likely than girls to be arrested for drug and alcohol abuse.*
- *Boys are 10 times more likely than girls to act out their pain by being violent toward others.*
- *Boys comprise 90 percent of the children who require school discipline.*
- *Boys commit nearly 93 percent of all juvenile murders.*

Experts have tried to unravel the causes of the mindless murders the boys committed. They have blamed video games, the media, drugs—both prescribed and illegal—permissive parents, music lyrics, and a host of other things. While any or all of these factors could have contributed to this rash of violence, few experts looked at the difference between the way boys and girls are raised. In studies observing little boys and little girls playing in the sandbox, it has been documented that different behaviors are encouraged for each gender. For example, if a little girl throws sand at a playmate, her mother scolds her to "play nice." But if a boy acts in a similarly aggressive way, his mother is more accepting of his behavior. As a college professor, I discussed these differences with a group of my students. A young father didn't believe me. He said he had both a little girl and a little boy, 3 and 4 years old, respectively. He insisted that his wife would never show such obvious favoritism. I encouraged him not to buy my words. I asked him instead to observe his kids' actions, and his wife's (and even his own) reactions the next time he watched them play.

The following week, my student returned to class and apologized. He said that he honestly couldn't imagine that a parent could raise two children so differently. But he said that he actually saw his wife *permitting* and *encouraging* his son's more aggressive behaviors, while she came down hard on his little daughter when she tried to do the same things!

There are many more differences in the way girls and boys are raised. Girls are allowed to cry as an outlet for feeling sad and depressed. Boys are told to "be a man," which means, "It's not okay to cry, but it is all right to show anger." In fact, boys are not allowed to even admit they feel depressed; that's a girl's thing. As a result, girls at 18 are twice as likely to be depressed as boys the same age. University of Michigan and Princeton University researchers asked adolescents what they worried about. Girls said looks, friends, family, self-worth, and safety, while boys said *performing* well in sports. When profiles were written about the perpetrators of the most recent violent school acts, it was discovered that each of the boys had been teased by classmates or rejected by girlfriends. Without an acceptable outlet for letting off steam—except anger, which spiraled out of control—these boys were unable to contain their feelings of being cut down.

If boys don't feel comfortable communicating their feelings, their anger has nowhere to go but to blow up in violence. True to their caveman ancestors, despite the antigun lobbyists, boys today are still encouraged to be hunters who use weapons. In fact, studies now point to 24 percent of male high school students admitting to carrying a weapon to school. I recently appeared on *Court TV* to comment on an unfolding murder trial. We observed how the accused murderer was raising his stepson. The 5-year-old boy often greeted his step-dad by pulling out his fake gun, aiming it at the man, and imitating a gun battle in the wild west. In turn, his stepfather would remove his own *real* gun, aim it at the child, and do the same thing. This was this family's *culture*, and a way that the two males demonstrated their love! If this is the best means of men showing love, our entire society needs an overhaul.

There are additional differences between the sexes. Directed from the right side of the brain, guys excel at spatial tasks, or activities that require the use of space, like building things, fixing cars, or playing ball. This is an important fact stemming back millions of years to when males went out to find the food and females stayed in the cave to raise the kids. Men were hunters, and hunting is a spatial task. When an animal moved through space, the caveman had to be successful in killing it to provide the food for his family. To be equipped to survive the difficulties of the hunt and the outdoors, men developed thick muscles and less body fat than women. This made them better able to use their aggressions and competitive instincts to outsmart the animals. Unlike females, they had no need to discuss their deep feelings or to speak about loving commitments.

We may be into a new millennium, but today's male behaviors have not changed much from those of millions of years ago. Men still hunt (check out the way they hunt for action and adventure with the remote control), and they'd rather perform spatial activities than talk about feelings and relationships, which women enjoy. For every one word a 12-year-old boy uses, a 12-year-old girl will use three to five. This lack of conversation frustrates the females who are involved with these guys. A wise girl understands what motivates male behaviors. She can laugh at some of their acting out as long as they're not acting out at her. She accepts their aggressiveness as a form of "physical communication," since they're pretty miserable at verbal communication. A smart girl will surely put a halt to any guy's actions that are violent. Ultimately, girls who have successful relationships have devised ways to get around men's age-old traits that sometimes perplex even the guys themselves.

So strong are the male's testosterone urges that, in a study conducted out of the University of Florida, it was found that 3 out of 4 males would say yes to sleeping with a strange woman. In contrast, the study also found that 100 percent of the females not only refused, but were downright offended by the offer. These finding show the different ways males and females react to the opportunity for casual sex. Males usually take advantage of almost any opportunity for sex.

Dear Dr. Gilda:

I'm seeing a girl I'm intimate with. But I'm not really "into" the relationship. It's not that I don't like her, it's just that she's just okay. Now this other girl wants to date me. I really like her. So I'm not sure how to handle it. I told the girl I'm seeing not to get attached to me. But she did. Am I making a mistake by 1) wanting to date this other girl and 2) seeing someone who I can't seem to put my heart into in a relationship? Please, please help me!   *Neil*

Dear Neil:

I receive lots of letters from girls who get hurt because their guy either ends up cheating on them openly, or sneaks around behind their backs with other girls. You obviously are sensitive enough to write to me about being conflicted. Good for you. A lot of guys would simply do what their hormones tell them to do. But you know that your "girlfriend" has feelings for you and is going to be hurt if you cheat. Apparently, even though you told her not to get attached to you, she did. She preferred to believe that since you two are intimate you have something special going on. It's not fair to her to continue like this. Sure, it's free sex for you without any strings on your part. But you're setting her up for a lot of pain. Is this what you want to do?

If your heart isn't in it as hers is, you're leading her on. The fairest thing for you to do now is to break up with her and let her go. This will allow you to be free to date anyone else you like, to feel as though you don't have to answer to a girlfriend, and to explore a relationship with someone you do care about when you're ready. Right now, perhaps you're just not ready for commitment. That's all right if your partner is okay with that, too.

The thing you should understand about girls is that many of them believe that no matter what a guy tells them, if he is having sex with them, he cares. Obviously, you know better. So be a cool guy and let this girl off the hook. She'll undoubtedly be upset at first, but in the long run, it's the right thing to do. And, in addition, you'll be in the experienced position of advising other guys who are in similar situations about what they should do.

On behalf of the entire female population, I thank you for your sincerity.   *Dr. Gilda*

Unlike their male counterparts, smart girls acknowledge that they have much at stake, and therefore take a cautious approach to having sex with a guy. When they do have sex, they want it to mean something. With more at stake, females are choosier about who they want as a boyfriend, so males have to work hard to get noticed. They strut their stuff and try to convince females to change their decisions from "no" to "yes." Guys may say "I love you" when they don't mean it, and they may make empty promises to get what they want. Girls must be aware that these guys are thinking with the wrong body parts ("with the wrong head," as 14-year-old Jana says) and if the girls want guys who are sincere, they'd better cool their jets before going off with a guy they hardly know.

I recently appeared on an NBC *Dateline* show to discuss the pros and cons of coed sleepovers for teenagers. Especially where kids are drinking and the hours are getting late, parents would rather have groups of teens sleep in the basement of one of their homes than to allow them to drive intoxicated. On the surface coed sleepovers seem like a safer choice. *Dateline* interviewed some very responsible-seeming high school kids and their parents, who said that their coed sleepovers were safe, fun events, and that there was no drinking or sex that went on because all the kids were "friends." I vehemently held a position that was unpopular with the teens: even if the kids were friends, the fact that young boys' hormones are spiking to new heights puts these teens at the unfair advantage of a) perhaps having to deal with their sexual urges in mixed company, and b) perhaps having to say 'no' to the pressure of a "friendly" come-on. My feeling is why set kids up for such pressure when it can be avoided? Teens today have enough stress to deal with. Of course, even if these young people have the greatest intentions, the truth is that boys start producing sperm at about 12 1/2 years old, they have at least a few erections while asleep (not to mention those they have while awake), and the number of sperm cells in an average ejaculation is 100 million. As a society, we complain about the problems of casual sex, STDs, and teen pregnancy. Why make those possibilities so easily available?

How to Trust Your Guy

A problem with teenage testosterone arises when a girl thinks she can count on a guy she likes, and she disappointingly finds out otherwise. A girl wants to believe a guy's promises that he cares for her and will be there for her emotionally and physically when she needs him. With testosterone surges, a once-dependable guy suddenly switches gears and becomes an aggressive freak that the girl doesn't even recognize. The girl becomes frustrated, she feels abandoned, and her trust disappears. If this happens often enough, a teenage girl's trust in guys erodes in general, and I receive letters like these:

> *Dear Dr. Gilda:*
>
> I have been dating my boyfriend for over three years. I love him, but I can't seem to trust him. He hasn't done anything for me not to trust him. But it's happened to me before. How do I learn to trust him before it's too late?   *Amy*

Dear Amy:

Your boyfriend is suffering the consequences of *your* past. Think of the guy who hurt you before. Then realize that he is not the same person as your boyfriend. Accept your boyfriend for the wonderful person he is without comparing him to any of your exes. Think often of his positive qualities and the reasons you hooked up with him in the first place. Remember that you've been together for a long three years. Certainly, he's got some great qualities. If you continue to concentrate on distrustful things you expect him to do, you are not being fair to him or to the relationship. Trust must begin somewhere. With the amount of time you've invested in your togetherness, now give him the benefit of the doubt. Otherwise you may lose him.

Dr. Gilda

When a girl accuses a guy of doing deeds he didn't do, she's in jeopardy of losing him. This is what is happening to Concerned after only two months:

Dear Dr. Gilda:

I've been dating this great guy for two months. When I'm not around him or don't know what he's doing, I get nervous thinking that he's cheating, even though he probably isn't. He gets mad when I accuse him. I try to trust, but it's hard. He's great and I love him. How do I learn to trust when I'm not with him?

Sincerely,
Concerned

Dear Concerned:

You are so right to recognize that this is a problem. Guys don't like to be accused of cheating, especially when they aren't. If you put cheating ideas in your boyfriend's head, who knows what weird way he'll react. I've heard teenage guys say, "Well, she thinks I'm cheating, she constantly nags me about doing it, so I might as well cheat. She thinks I'm doing it anyway." You don't want this to happen to you.

Your distrust is coming from your feelings of insecurity about this guy and about the relationship. It's only been two months and you're still getting to know each other. If he's a cool guy, over time he will give you reason to feel more secure.

Meanwhile, have a heart-to-heart with your guy and honestly share your feelings. Ask him to help you feel more secure by calling you more often and proving to you he really does care. Tell him that that will make you feel a whole lot better.

Of course, if he denies your wishes, that will tell you a lot about his character and about how little he cares for you. Keep in mind that some guys actually want their girlfriends to think of them as desirable to other girls, so they go out of their way to try to make them jealous. They need lots of girls to stroke their egos, but no girl should have to be a party to this kind of immaturity. If that's the case, this guy is a loser who deserves to be lost!

Dr. Gilda

Sometimes, testosterone surges cause guys to stupidly show off. But while they're in the "high" of their show-off moment, they may embarrass their girlfriend. Eventually, if a guy continues to embarrass her, she will lose trust in him. Once trust is lost, it is hard to get back. Building and rebuilding trust takes time, as Heather will attest to:

Dear Dr. Gilda:

I love my boyfriend to death, but he did something that made me lose my trust in him. It's been awhile and I want to know how I can get that trust back. I think this is the guy I want to marry someday. Help!   *Heather*

Dear Heather:

Be open with your guy and tell him how you feel. He will need to bend over backward to prove to you that you can trust him, but these are the consequences of stupid actions. Whatever you do, don't even think of marrying him until this trust issue is resolved. A mar-

> riage based on *dis*trust can never survive. In fact, if you
> don't resolve this issue now, your negative feelings
> toward your guy will only worsen as he continues to
> disappoint you. You don't need a divorce before you
> get a marriage!
>   *Dr. Gilda*

It may have been his hot bod that turned you on when you
first met him, or his silly smile, his great sense of humor, or
even his fine threads. But over time, relationships go deeper
than these superficial attractions. As you can see from all my
responses to these letters, communicating honestly with your
boyfriend is key to keeping love alive beyond the initial thrill.
If you feel that your guy is not receptive to your baring your
soul, or is not sensitive to your special feelings, it's best you discover that now, before your heart gets smashed to smithereens.

Of course, there are usually good reasons for a girl not
trusting guys in general. Michelle describes how being raped
two years before meeting Juan set the stage for her to distrust
all men:

> *Dear Dr. Gilda:*
>   I have a little problem. I'm 16 years old and living in
> a small town in Texas. I have been talking to this guy
> for quite some time and I feel like I'm getting closer and
> closer to him every day. At first, when we started talk-
> ing, I really didn't want to get close to him because of

my past. I was raped when I was 14, and I had a few boyfriends that have hit me. So when I started talking to Juan, I wanted to take everything slow.

Although we have known each other for a year, we've been talking seriously for six months. We were always good friends. Juan had always wanted a relationship with me but I never gave him the time of day. My problem is that now I know how to be in a relationship with him, but I'm scared that I won't be able to trust him. I told him that is the only reason I can't go out with him. I'm so scared about trusting a guy that I can't even trust my own father and brother, not that they have ever done anything to me not to be able to trust them. It's just that I can't trust any man. I want to be able to trust Juan.

Should I be able to trust him now (considering that he has never done anything to hurt me and I feel that I am in love) or should I just call it off? Shouldn't I be able to forget about the past? Or should I hide in the bushes for the rest of my life?

Thanks a lot,
Michelle

Dear Michelle:

My dear, with all you've been through it's no wonder that trust would be a big issue for you. You should know this sorry statistic:

Gilda Gram   One quarter of all teenage girls experience dating violence.

What's more, the majority of dating violence occurs when a relationship is a serious, steady one. It's a horrible thought that girls who are out on dates with guys they presumably know and trust end up being violated. But for you now to think that the only way around this is to "hide in the bushes" for the rest of your life is simply being unfair to yourself.

Before you do another thing, find a female counselor who specializes in rape issues. You will also want to find out how you attracted the guys who ended up hitting you. You are only 16 with a whole life ahead of you. For starters, if you don't handle your past, you'd be denying both yourself and Juan the opportunity of trying to enjoy a future together. Even if the relationship with Juan doesn't work out, you must be able to put this bad experience behind you so that another, perhaps even better, union is possible. You deserve to have a happy life. Give yourself the gift of therapy—and hope—that will lead you to a glorious future.   *Dr. Gilda*

Yes, trust takes time. Two people must get to know each other, seeing each other when things are good, but also experiencing the times when life is not so sweet. Girls should see their boyfriend being sad, upset, and angry, and they must notice how he deals with situations that don't go his way. As a couple gets to live through each other's school, family, and work pressures, they get to know each other well. But even when you think you really know someone, sometimes you're suddenly shocked by a new, "strange" behavior:

Dear Dr. Gilda:

I am from West Virginia. I am 17 years old and I need your help really bad!!! Well, I have this boyfriend and we have been dating for almost two years. Lately, we have been arguing and fighting over stupid things like me talking to one of his "ex-friends," as he calls him. The other day he threw a chair and broke it because he got mad at me. Then a week after that he hit the bathroom door and put a hole in it about one inch from my head. He said he was mad at me again. I thought I loved him, but now I'm not sure. What do I do? Would you please help me? I am really confused.

Candy

Dear Candy:

It's no wonder you're confused. You thought you knew this guy fairly well, and now it seems he's blowing his cork each time he becomes frustrated with something you do. He must get help at once. But until he does, steer clear of him. So far, he's only done harm to objects. When tempers flare, a person can totally lose control of his thoughts and actions to the point of his hurting people around him.

For your own safety, you've got to stay away. Perhaps he needs to be on medication, or maybe he needs to attend anger-management classes. He must speak to a therapist and determine the cause of his sudden behavioral outbursts. But whatever he does, you've got to protect yourself. So tell him you're freeing yourself of him until he takes care of his problem. If he tells you he doesn't have a problem, stay away indefinitely.

Dr. Gilda

Because it takes awhile until someone feels comfortable enough to reveal his true personality, I advise teens not to jump into steady relationships too soon. If they do, they may find that they got involved too quickly with someone they really don't know, who ends up hurting them badly. Many of the trust issues I encounter with teens could be prevented if only these kids would take their time.

When does distrust end and real trust begin?

Gilda Gram   Trust begins by trusting your own judgment.

Because guys are taught that emotions are wussy, girls are far more likely to depend on their intuition. They are usually able to quickly perceive the real meaning behind a guy's actions. On some level, most of us can usually tell when a guy's only interested in a fling. Even if we choose to ignore the obvious signals, we know when someone is no good for us and will not make good boyfriend material. For example, Brittany *already knows* that this guy she calls her "boyfriend" should not be a keeper:

> *Dear Dr. Gilda:*
>
> I have a problem. My boyfriend asked me out because he and his friends made a bet that they have to ask someone. I'm not sure if he really likes me because he rarely ever calls me and he flirts with my friends.
>
> *Brittany*
>
> *Dear Brittany:*
>
> Come on, girl. You don't need me to tell you what you already know. This guy is more devoted to his pals than to you. Find someone who genuinely wants to be with you without his immature friends daring him to. And if he's so intent on flirting with other girls, you surely don't need him flirting with you!   *Dr. Gilda*

Brittany's dilemma is obvious. Of course, it's still early in the game for this pair, and it doesn't even sound as though she should be calling him her "boyfriend." But what if she's one of those girls who refuses to heed the blaring signs that this guy will turn into a heart-crusher? What if she continues to crush on this "boyfriend" and will not stop until the signals hit her over the head? Girls I've interviewed who've experienced the heartbreak of being with a cheater have named some of the signs that will help you wise up.

Telltale Signs Your Guy's a Two-timer

If you are a girl who even suspects that her man is carrying on elsewhere, note some of the more obvious telltale signs:

1. He *suddenly* alters the way he dresses and smells. All of a sudden your guy is dousing himself with so much cologne he attracts insects. He has added new jewelry, a different look to his style of clothes, and a new haircut.
2. He *suddenly* alters his usual behavior, either presenting you with lots of gifts, flowers, and affection when he's never behaved this way before, or, if he has been generous with these, he suddenly cuts off the supply of goodies that usually shows he cares.
3. His technology habits are *suddenly* different. His beeper goes off with unfamiliar numbers, he begins to conceal his answering machine messages, and he purposely doesn't answer his phone when you're around.
4. He constantly breaks dates, offering lame excuses that don't add up.

If you are experiencing any of these cheating clues, get wise! A girl doesn't need to be with a jerk who doesn't appreciate her. If he'd rather get his ego massaged by other skirts, it's time to pack him in. It's better to be alone than to be with a cheat. Eventually, you will meet someone who can make a commitment and keep it. There are plenty of cool guys out there, but you'll have to be in a position to recognize their great qualities when they're around you.

Talk about two-timers! I received a disturbing letter from a testosterone-crazed guy who admitted he needed my help:

Hey Doc,

I don't know why I do this to myself, but I'm falling for this girl, Mary. She is the girl I have been waiting for my whole life. She is 18, 5'11", 150 pounds, very sweet and innocent (she's still a virgin!), and gorgeous. She played basketball in high school but doesn't love the game anymore. She runs every morning and the only bad thing is that she has a boyfriend. I honestly don't know what to do.

The past few nights I have been up in her dorm room just hanging out and talking. She told me on numerous occasions that I'm special and that I'm a really great guy and that whoever I'm with is a lucky girl. (I didn't tell her about Jenni, my girlfriend back home, but she knows about the girl I'm sleeping with in college, Valori.) She is just so damn adorable. She calls me Richard (instead of Rick) and I have a nickname for her and she said that I'm the only one allowed to use it. It's "Cheeks" because she has the most adorable cheeks when she smiles. They come up and I pinch them and she just giggles.

Man, I don't know what to do. Should I distance

myself from her to let my feelings cool down, should I pursue her, or should I just chill? What, what, what?

Ben

Dear Ben,

You are really something! You have a girl back home (who's probably waiting patiently for you), you have one you're sleeping with in college, and now you want to have "the girl of your dreams" who you've waited for your "whole life"!

My friend, you're not being fair to any of these women. Frankly, if they're stupid enough to go for your fickle affections, they deserve you. If you have any decency, you'll leave Mary alone. You can be her friend, but forget about trespassing on another's guy's territory. Besides, it sounds like you'd get bored with her as soon as she was really yours. Your biggest commitment right now should be to yourself. You should take the time to grow up before you break any more hearts.

Dr. Gilda

No doubt, self-involved Ben feels that his confusion is driving him crazy. Little does he care about what it's doing to the girls he's hurting.

You've learned the traits that make a guy cool. Now practice assessing the guys you know who you might never even have thought about as boyfriend material. The more you rate different personalities correctly, the more you should compliment yourself on your keen ability to trust your heart. The more capable you are to know which sweeties to keep around, the better you'll be at dumping the bummers.

> **Gilda Gram**   Be your own guy-ger counter. Trust your ability to keep the best and dump the rest.

So what's a good girl to do about the natural impulses that overwhelm the body of a teenage guy? Surely she can't help what's going on inside him, nor is she responsible for his acting-out aggression. In short, unless his behavior threatens her safety or reputation, it is not her concern. After thoroughly understanding what guys this age are all about, the best protection you can have is:

> **Gilda Gram**   Get to know a guy for a while before you decide to hook up.

Getting to know someone well allows him to also get to know you as a person and as a friend. Once he begins to see you as someone he doesn't take for granted, he'll treat you with respect. Keep in mind that his testosterone surges will still overwhelm him. Therefore, be prepared to check out your boyfriend's behavior to see whether his macho feelings have gone to his head and have taken him over completely.

Testosterone Tester

1. Does he think he's Rocky and can take on the world?
2. Does he believe he's better than everyone else?
3. Does he think it's okay for him to be flirting with other chicas even though you're by his side?

If you answer yes to any of these, you might want to reconsider how great you think your guy really is. Audrey found herself stumped as to what was happening to her boyfriend of a few months:

> *Dear Dr. Gilda:*
>
> I need a lot of help! My boyfriend is turning out to be another guy, if you know what I mean. He's usually wonderful toward me, but out of blue, he'll start flirting with other girls right in front of me as though I'm not even there. We get into fights a lot as a result. What can I do?
>
> He knows this is destroying me. I've tried not to get mad, but it's so hard seeing everything I have a problem with being done right before my eyes. On these occasions, it seems that he doesn't care if he makes me mad. Then later, he'll act like nothing at all happened. How can I look past his behavior and try to change my feelings? I don't want to let him go. He means too much to me.
>
> *Audrey, 16*

Dear Audrey:

Your boyfriend's testosterone surges might explain his sudden changed behavior. However, just because you understand his behavior doesn't mean that you have to put up with being dissed. What disturbed me most about your letter is your question about how to "look past his behavior and try to change your feelings." You have a right to your feelings, and you never want to change them. In fact, feelings serve a good purpose. They are an alarm that tells you that you're not being respected and that you feel awful about it. They alert you to communicate with your guy about your feelings regarding his poor treatment of you.

After you confront your guy, he may be totally dense and not understand what you're talking about. If he chooses not to curb his aggressions, he's telling you a lot about how little you mean to him. While you say that you don't want to let him go, you're right in your statement that he means *too much* to you. Nobody should mean so much to someone that she disregards her feelings. You deserve to be cherished by your boyfriend. If this guy will not adore you, find someone who will.

Dr. Gilda

While guys have testosterone surges, girls experience their own hormonal changes. This occurs when they get their periods, as I discussed earlier. If each time a girl menstruates, her guy goes off muttering, "The bitch is back"—and he's right—you know he won't hang around too long, will he? And why should he? Just because our body occasionally goes out of whack is no excuse for us to be disrespectful to people we supposedly care for. While we can certainly benefit from the information that tells us why we act the way we act, it does not give us license to mistreat someone. This goes for both sexes. If you are being dissed by the guy who has pledged to love you, stop right now and examine the way you feel about his behavior. After confronting him in a calm and open way, if he still refuses to curb his aggressive outbursts, your best option is to take care of yourself by walking away. Whether you return to him can be determined after you've both had a break from each other.

In the meantime, if your dude's moods continue to be an issue for you in the relationship, do a mood check on him to determine whether you want to keep him hanging on:

Check the Mood of Your Dude

Does your guy have his two feet solidly planted on the ground, or does he often swing into the king of conceit? Place a Yes or No beside each of the following questions to get a read on his level of aggressiveness. Obviously, mucho macho can destroy his relationship with you.

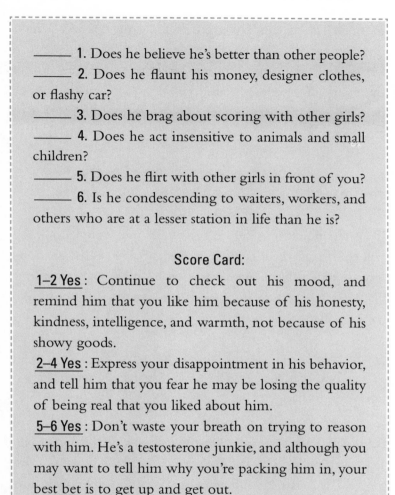

—— 1. Does he believe he's better than other people?

—— 2. Does he flaunt his money, designer clothes, or flashy car?

—— 3. Does he brag about scoring with other girls?

—— 4. Does he act insensitive to animals and small children?

—— 5. Does he flirt with other girls in front of you?

—— 6. Is he condescending to waiters, workers, and others who are at a lesser station in life than he is?

Score Card:

<u>1–2 Yes</u> : Continue to check out his mood, and remind him that you like him because of his honesty, kindness, intelligence, and warmth, not because of his showy goods.

<u>2–4 Yes</u> : Express your disappointment in his behavior, and tell him that you fear he may be losing the quality of being real that you liked about him.

<u>5–6 Yes</u> : Don't waste your breath on trying to reason with him. He's a testosterone junkie, and although you may want to tell him why you're packing him in, your best bet is to get up and get out.

When a girl hooks up with a guy, just like when she hooks up with girlfriends, she should be sure that he *enhances* the way she already feels about herself. If you have followed the beginning chapters of this book carefully, you know that you must feel good about yourself before you connect with a guy romantically. When a girl feels confident, whenever a guy's surges bring out his fangs, she can go off and do her thing, and if necessary, stand her ground when he tries to dominate her. But remember that you are not his mother or teacher:

> **Gilda Gram**   Girls don't have to educate guys. They just have to not buy into their nonsense.

If a girl's not strong before she enters into coupledom, she will continually be disappointed and unhappy as the relationship unfolds and the guy does what his biology dictates—no matter what she tells him about her needs. A girl must feel emotionally safe. In other words,

> **Gilda Gram**   If you don't feel safe with him, don't get hooked on him.

Remember, boys are raised to think they must be aggressive. They are taught to be the hunters who call the shots. We saw some of the names of fragrances that pressure females into finding Romance and being Happy. Look at two of the names of fragrances that pressure guys to live up to being he-men: Goodlife and Pleasures. In other words, the ads tell them to get what they can get to live the good life, and while they're at it, be sure they derive plenty of pleasure! That's a lot of pressure for guys. What's more, the female gender is a mystery to them. Like their cavemen ancestors, their mission is to find adventure in the wild. This romance stuff is way beyond anything they're familiar with. This quality in guys is very frustrating for the girls who like them. In order to get through to guys they like and win their hearts, girls often wind up doing things they are sorry for later.

What I Do for Love

Guys may seem hardheaded when it comes to romance, but they aren't dumb. Many of them need help and coaxing to get out the words of caring. And even though they might end up taking some ribbing from their buddies, most of them want to feel close to someone as much as girls do.

Do you think that guys have easier lives than girls? What would happen if you woke up one morning as a guy? How would you handle it? Complete the following sentence with whatever comes to mind: "If I woke up as a boy, . . ." In a collection of responses from different high school girls, some answers were:

1. I'd pee standing up.
2. I'd take off my shirt and swim.
3. I'd burn my pads and throw away my Midol.
4. I'd walk around in just boxers.
5. I'd do my hair without gel.
6. I'd scratch my balls.
7. I'd burn my bras.

While these responses might not seem earth-shattering, they show the effort girls put into the daily course of being feminine. They walk around worried that their hair isn't perfect, their makeup isn't right, their clothes aren't "in." Even if they already have a boyfriend, they constantly feel the pressure to impress. One girl in a relationship for three months revealed, "If I'm in a bad mood, I'll scream, yell, and curse with my girlfriends, but when I'm around Carl, I refrain from acting upset." So, in other words, as soon as guys enter the picture: lights, camera, action . . . a new self!! Too many girls become boy-pleasers to the point that it is nauseating. They cook and bake for him, they overapologize, they always make themselves available, they inconvenience themselves to please him, they have trouble telling him no, and their own needs and goals take a backseat to those of their boyfriend. Especially upsetting was a recent news article regarding 13- and 14-year-old teenage girls in a Virginia middle school who were giving guys oral sex. The girls named the act "a popularity kind of thing," and agreed that such hooking up could last a couple of weeks or only a few hours. Unfortunately, while the guys asked the girls to perform this act on them because they thought the girls were hot, the girls wanted to have full-blown relationships. What actually happened was that the boys received sexual gratification, and the girls felt demeaned. Why do girls do this to themselves? To impress guys, to get their attention, and to win their love.

Fitting in is one of the greatest challenges teens have. In a *USA Today* panel of twenty-five teenage members, the consensus is that the "cool" crowd is often defined by money.

Money buys the best clothes, cell phone, Palm Pilot, and car, and there is an implication that you are not a significant person unless you sport the right brands. For a lot of girls, sporting the right brands attracts the "in crowd" guys. At first, a girl feels delighted to be let in. But after a while, the downside of blind belonging begins to take its toll. It's dangerous to enact behavior that makes you feel uncomfortable because you want to belong, but it's just as dangerous to belong and then lose your identity. Resisting peer pressure may be tough, but it's even tougher after you find yourself in a bind because your allegiance had been to your friends instead of to your own values.

Here's a news flash: No girl has to put out to fit in. In fact, any girl who does is putting herself down. Susan went to a party and met Bernard. They hooked up immediately. But as soon as they did, and they kissed, Susan thought that Bernard was a bad kisser. But she rationalized, "He's really nice, and he really likes me. So I'll stay with him tonight because I feel obligated." Susan stayed with Bernard the entire night at the party and maybe even missed out on meeting someone she liked better. But she said that she didn't want him to feel that she was just using him. She said that she felt she had to stay because she'd be called a bitch if she just kissed him and left him. I said, "Where is your obligation to yourself?" Susan couldn't answer because she didn't know. If Susan had been an It Girl, she would have known that she must honor her rights to herself as Number One.

Sometimes the stories I hear go a lot further than just hooking up and kissing. That was the case with Therese.

Dear Dr. Gilda:

I'm 14 and pregnant with my ex's baby. After we had sex everything changed. He acted real different toward me. Before that time, he was sweet, and seemed to really care. Now I don't know what to do. Please help!   *Therese*

Dear Therese:

I'm afraid it's too late for me to tell you the sad statistic that 90 percent of the males who impregnate a teenage girl abandon her and her family. You must find an adult you can trust, and weigh all your alternatives with that person. This must serve as a learning experience for you, so that you don't find yourself in the same predicament in the future.   *Dr. Gilda*

There is controversy about the kind of message being taught today in sex education programs across the country. According to the Alan Guttmacher Institute, abstinence is advocated by 86 percent of school districts. In another survey, the Kaiser Family Foundation finds that 94 percent of high school sex ed classes tell students to just say no to intercourse until they feel they are emotionally ready or married. Most of these programs totally omit information about birth control and safe sex methods. Because many teens find it unrealistic that abstinence is the only option available, they completely disregard the message that they must be careful about their sexual partners—and unfortunately end up like Therese. It's very upsetting to receive e-mail like this, after it's too late, because at that point, all I can advise is that the girl get help from an adult who can assist her with tough decisions. No matter what decision she reaches, it will be a trying and crying time of crisis and pain.

Therese found out that having a guy is not as important as it may seem if it means altering the rest of her life. Before any girl commits her body to a guy, she'd better be absolutely sure that he has committed his soul to her!

Gilda Gram   Finding a boyfriend is not a gotta-get-it goal.

When a girl becomes so boy-crazy that she puts a guy on a pedestal and loses herself to him, she gives away her individuality. Not treating yourself like Number One only brings you disrespect. And disrespect can make a girl feel worse than she felt when she was without a guy!

He May Be Aggressive, but He Still Wants Love

If you don't believe that guys want love as much as girls do, look at just some of the letters I've received from the male species. The writers range in ages from 14 to 20. It's startling to realize that guys want caring the same as you do, although they don't seem as compassionate as you in their attempts to get it.

Dear Dr. Gilda:

This may sound weird, but how do I get a girl to like me?   *Luke, 14*

Dear Dr. Gilda:

There's a friend who I have known for about three years who I really love. She doesn't know how I feel. I have tried to tell her a few times, but every time I try, I chicken out. Any suggestions?   *Tortured, age 15*

Dear Dr. Gilda:

My girlfriend and I have been broken up for about a week now and I still love her so much! Since Valentine's Day is coming up, what should I give her so she would know that I love her?   *H.H., age 16*

Dear Dr. Gilda:

Well, I just asked out this girl who I liked for a long time. I had given her a rose and it was really sweet, but that is the trouble. I want to be the sweetest and best man she has ever known. I am not sure what things I should do.   *Tim, 17 years old*

Dear Dr. Gilda:

I've never been in love before. I recently met someone who is perfect for me. The thing is, she doesn't want to get very serious with me, or apparently anyone, because her last relationships ended badly. I've made my feelings clear to her. We've only been out a few times so maybe it's too early for her to decide. How should I go about convincing her without making her feel rushed or pressured?   *Bob, 18*

Dear Dr. Gilda:

I am wondering if you can tell me what is most likely going on in my ex-girlfriend's head to hurt me the way she has. Let me give you a little background information. My ex and I have been together for three years, since she was not even 14 and I was 16. We became really close quickly and had been great friends for these past few years. But things suddenly changed. My brother started bringing around a friend who took a liking to my girlfriend. We would all hang out together drinking every night when I noticed that all my girlfriend and that kid did was talk by themselves. Then I started noticing eye contact and smiles. They would follow each other to the bathroom and take longer than they should to return. This all went on in my own house.

I took this kid in as a friend and actually took him on vacation with us. My girl and I probably had 20 to 30 fights about him and she told me that I was crazy for even suggesting that they liked each other. Love-blind me believed her. Two months ago we decided that we needed space. Now she says that her feelings have changed for me because I treated her badly. I don't deny that I did do some bad things, but I promised her that I was willing to do my part and change. She tells me she needs time to straighten her head out and that I should stop begging her to come back because she is looking at me as a weak person that she could never be with. She tells me that she needs time to miss me. Will she ever wake up? She's the one who begged me to put a ring on her finger. What is she doing now? She has turned my world upside down.

Broken up,
Les, 19

Dear Dr. Gilda:

I have a problem. I've been really good friends with this girl for about a year. We have always been attracted to each other, and she finally broke up with her boyfriend. We slept with each other about a week later, and it totally changed our relationship, as I knew it would. She is now back with her man and I don't know what to do. She is still attracted to me, and says she would break up with her man for me when I come back from college. (I am leaving for college in California for two years. She wants me to come back to Arizona and marry her!) There is a slight problem: age. She is 17 and I am 20. I don't know if it is her immaturity or what, but this has been on my mind for a long time and I really do have strong feelings for her. Please help!?!

Al, 20

Not only do boys want love as much as girls do, their feelings are just as sensitive. They want to find answers to their love problems but they don't know who to ask. I receive a lot of e-mail over the Internet from boys because this medium allows them to be anonymous and keep their egos intact. If they talk to their buds they'll be ostracized and teased. If they talk to a gal pal they run the risk of gossip. If they reveal their true emotions to the girl they like, they're afraid of rejection. So without knowing who to trust and how to behave, they end up acting stupid and looking foolish. Or, they act disinterested, giving the impression that they couldn't care less.

Unacceptable Behavior from Guys

The overriding lesson girls must understand is that no matter how sensitive a boy is, or how stupidly he behaves, the only thing that counts is how he behaves toward her. Sometimes, she may have to get him alone for his real caring self to come out. But if he's rude and disrespectful in front of others, no matter how much good she sees in him deep beneath the surface when his friends are not around, he's a loser. She should immediately tell him she will not accept this treatment. If her words go in one ear and out the other, and he continues to diss her, he needs to be dumped.

Elaine learned early on that Marc was not someone she could count on. Yet she still liked him in some way, and she felt ambivalent about wanting him as a boyfriend, sometimes telling herself yes and other times telling herself no. The two of them were having one of their typical flirting sessions one day after school:

Marc: "So when are you gonna give me head?"

Elaine (Laughs): "Oh, Marc, stop it."

Marc: "Are you coming home on the bus?"

Elaine: "Yes."

Marc: "Good. We can get started right away."

Elaine enjoyed the attention Marc was paying her, and she never considered that the way Marc was speaking to her was disrespectful. When I raised the issue with her and told her that she should not allow boys to speak to her in dirty ways, she admitted that she "sort of" knew that. When I asked her why she puts up with it, she answered, "Aside from his horniness, he's a good friend. He just sometimes thinks with his other head. He's so sweet when he's not horny. We talk. He gives me advice. He wants sex, but he doesn't want to go out with me. I really don't get it." Secretly, Elaine wished that Marc would ask her out to prove that he liked her as more than just a friend. Yet she came to recognize that that was clearly not Marc's intention. Apparently, he enjoyed their friendship, but that was a separate issue for him. He wasn't looking for a steady girlfriend. He just wanted a girl to have sex with, true to the model of the testosterone-crazed teenage boy. Fortunately, Elaine vowed that she was not going to be that girl.

The fact that Elaine was willing to play along in the flirtation proved how wishy-washy she was about her feelings toward this guy. "Sort of" knowing that she was being disrespected, she still tried to laugh it off. She also knew that if she agreed to do it, Marc would have sex with her in a minute. But even though she had hoped it would be different, she also knew that he really wasn't interested in her as a girlfriend. And that was Elaine's condition for getting sexually close to a guy.

Unlike a lot of girls, Elaine is smart enough not to try to trick herself into believing that Marc cares for her. However, she's also not confident enough to tell him to flake off. So she continues her part in the flirting game, while both of them get positive feelings from the attention they're giving each other.

In contrast, "Helpless" is not getting any positive feelings at all from the guy she's crushing on. In fact, she's a glutton for punishment as she continues to try to win her crush's attentions no matter how rude he is to her:

Dear Dr. Gilda:

I went out with a guy last year for a few months and we broke up. I have liked one of his friends for a long time but all he does is call me rude names. I think it is because my ex-boyfriend tells him to say dirty things to me. How can I get him to like me as a friend or maybe more? I have tried and tried to be nice, but he won't try back!

Helpless, 15

Dear Helpless:

The signature you use tells me a lot about you. "Helpless" makes you sound as though you have no say in this game of mean. For one thing, recognize that this guy is a jerk if he's acting only on the advice of your ex-boyfriend. You deserve to have a boyfriend who can think for himself. But even if he's thinking on his own that it's okay to say mean things to you, why would you want to keep such a fool around? Do you find a guy calling you rude names attractive? And you keep trying to get him to want you! Get a life!! You deserve someone who treats you well and respects you. Find a respectful couple and check out how they speak to each other and how the guy treats the girl. Then you'll see how nice it can be. Tell yourself that you deserve more, and don't settle for anything but the best treatment from a boy. Besides all this, I hope you recognize that no matter what anyone calls you, you know the truth. And that's that you're a terrific person as you are!

Dr. Gilda

The idea that a guy thinks that he can call a girl names and she'll believe them is mind-boggling. Yet I receive a lot of correspondence from young women who are quite upset with the name-calling. The old children's chant of "Sticks and stones will break your bones, but names will never harm you" is just not true. Names do hurt—if you give yourself permission to believe them.

Dear Dr. Gilda:

I just broke up with my baby's father and he says I can't get anyone else. Now I can't eat or sleep, and I don't want to go anywhere. What should I do?   *Cara*

Dear Cara:

There's only one thing you must do, and that is not to believe any of the names your baby's father calls you. The moment you allow his words to destroy you, that's the moment you give him total control over your life. It's time to release the spell he has over you, and tell yourself some positive things about how wonderful you are!   *Dr. Gilda*

Since a teenage guy's hormones often rule him, a girl must look out for her own best interests and rule herself. She must decide whether she's getting enough caring from the guy she's involved with. If she is, it may be worth her effort to put up with the guy's aggressive side of his personality when it emerges. But at any time, if the guy is benefiting from the relationship at the girl's expense, as hard as it may seem, she's got to let him go.

Dear Dr. Gilda:

I am 17 years old, and I have a 5 month-old baby girl by this guy I've been with for two years. He and I have had a very abusive relationship and he is always putting me down. He hit me and put me down for the last time. I finally called the cops on him. He is now on the run from them. He always calls and stops by, not to see his daughter, but to have sex and be mean to me. I don't know why I kept on letting him do this to me. I have to beg him to see his daughter and hold her and play with her, but he doesn't. Then he says I am taking him away from his little girl.

Now I find that I can't trust any man. Yet I still want him. What is wrong with me? Please help me get over him. He is driving me crazy. I think about him all the time. I can't eat, sleep, or be happy. I am a very good mom and I work two jobs and go to school. I don't want to go anywhere with any guys or anything. Help!!! Please, what should I do to get my life back together? I saw you on TV and you are beautiful!! I know you can help me.
                                                    Cookie

Dear Cookie:

Let this guy go!! You have been allowing yourself to be taken in by this guy's charms. Except for one fact:

he's not very charming. A guy who puts you down and hits you is totally out of control. When someone is out of control, they use their hands. That's not a man. That's a scared animal who feels he has to use force to get what he wants. You're trying to make something of your life by improving yourself in school and working. You sound like a terrific and responsible mother. But you're not being the best mother you can be if you allow your little girl to observe a woman who's a punching bag for a guy.

No doubt, you're bonded to this guy by your child. You've also spent two years of your life with him, with a lot of experiences. Of course you feel close to him. But he's toxic for both you and your child. Is this what you want your little girl to see? Is this how you want her to think all men treat women?

Tell yourself you deserve a man to love you in a positive way. Tell yourself you'll accept only the very best treatment. Tell yourself you'd rather be alone than be with an abuser. You must never again allow yourself to be alone with him. Always have another adult present to ensure your safety. Domestic violence usually occurs with people we know and who profess their love for us. This is how a lot of women get murdered. Your daughter needs you. Don't let her become one of those horrible statistics.

Dr. Gilda

Girls Can Be Aggressive, Too

Our culture adapts to the changing behaviors of the two genders. The last few years have seen girls become more aggressive, while guys have become more sensitive. This may be a good change because it takes some of the pressure off the guys to be in constant control, while it motivates girls to be more independent and assertive about seeking and satisfying their goals.

Yet no matter what societal changes occur, girls' brains produce more serotonin than guys' brains. Serotonin is a brain chemical that inhibits aggressive behavior. So while girls may think it's all right to stand up to their men when they're being abused, they still feel like shrinking violets when they have to do it. The same thing happens when girls want to ask guys out. They have reservations about what might happen if the guy turns them down. Of course, nobody wants to be rejected. But the serotonin helps explain why girls can be so ambivalent about their aggressions. A lot of the e-mail I receive from girls reads like this:

Dear Dr. Gilda:

I really like this guy and I think he might like me. I want to ask him out but I am afraid of being rejected. Many smart, beautiful, and nice girls have asked him out, including my best friend, and he turned every one of them down. What do you think is his problem?

Real Interested, 15

Dear Real Interested:

Maybe this guy is afraid of aggressive girls. If you really want to get close to a guy, begin by establishing a friendship with him. Then if any asking is to occur, he will feel comfortable doing it himself. Naturally, that lets you off the hook of feeling rejected. But also recognize that it's possible that he's into other things right now like school, sports, or earning money, and not girls. You can't make someone want you or be ready to care for you. If the timing is not right, there's nothing you can do about it. But you can surely try to interest him by being your sweet real self. If you don't pursue the friendship, you'll never know.   *Dr. Gilda*

Speaking of girls who allow their aggressions to run wild, I receive many letters from young women who think they have to act like men in combat:

Dear Dr. Gilda:

Hi! I have been seeing a guy for three months and the last man I broke up with . . . let's just say didn't last too long. I was at the movies with my friends when he and my male best friend were there. My best friend said they were meeting a girl that liked him (my best friend) and they were going as a gay couple. I knew something was up because my boy at the time wouldn't do that.

Well, I saw him with a girl. He didn't know I was watching (actually snooping). The girl he was with kept looking at me. I said to my friend, "I'll be back." I walked up to her and said that if she didn't stop giggling and staring at me I would deck her in the face. My former man put his head down and covered his face. Well, I got kicked out of the movies because the girl tested me and, well, I hit her and she bled. I know that was wrong. I am sorry for that.

I want to stay with my current boyfriend, but sometimes I want to go back to my ex. I made the mistake of asking my ex out this morning, and he said he'd get back to me. I have gotten myself into the biggest craphole now. Can you give me ANY advice?

I have read all your articles in *Teen Magazine* and I see you TV. I love your advice. I think my boyfriend really cares about me. But one reason I don't want to stay with him is because he wants to spend every waking moment with me and I don't want that! We know a lot about each other, and we're real compatible. My ex and I are also so compatible. My mom says this is all normal. My question is, why is this happening?

Cassie, 15
Hurt and Confused

Dear Cassie:

I bet you're hurt and confused! Your mom's right: your changing tastes in guys is normal for your age.

You're back and forth between these two guys because you haven't decided who you are and what you want. And it's also normal for you to want to flee from the guy who wants to own you 24/7. That's not a healthy relationship for either of you. You will find that you will probably be compatible with lots of guys before you settle down, so date lots of guys until you find someone you really love.

But most of all, NEVER use physical force on anyone to prove your point. If anything, it was you who looked like a jerk. Apparently, your ex was embarrassed by your outrageous behavior, and if you thought this was the way to win his heart, you were dead wrong. If your ex didn't want to be with this girl, he wouldn't have been there. And it's a free country for anyone to look at you and yes, even giggle, if they want to.

You know you were wrong, and that is good. Start working on your own problems before you try to find a guy.

Dr. Gilda

Some girls need my encouragement for them to take the reins. Toni, however, was not one of them. The only problem was, once she had them, she didn't know what to do with them:

Dear Dr. Gilda:

There's this boy in my class, Shawn. He is hot, and I want to date him. I am not sure if he likes me or how to tell him that I like him. But to stir things up a bit, I've been playing footsy with him! What should I do next?

Toni, 12

Dear Toni:

Take your free foot and use it to step on the one that's rubbing against Shawn. Try getting to know this guy for a while before you push the physical on him. This way, if there's even a chance he might be interested, he won't be frightened off by your "putting your best foot" forward. Some young guys fear that if a girl comes on strong at first, she'll eventually try to control them. Then their friends will call them "whipped." A lot of guys will do anything to protect themselves from being controlled by a girl. Take your time, let the relationship unfold if it's going to, and let Shawn think that it was he who did the hunting.

Dr. Gilda

Girls' Aggressions That Are Taken Too Far

Because of their new role as independent and assertive females, some girls don't quite know where to stop. At a wealthy New York private school, some sixth-grade girls were found developing a private sign language to taunt their peers and cast "spells" on those they disliked. This kind of teasing is mean-spirited and it hurts the girls on the receiving end. But it doesn't compare with some of the dangerous crimes committed by girls nationwide, as reported in the *New York Post* for the years between 1981 and 1997:

- *Arrest rates for girls increased more than for boys in every crime category in the United States.*
- *Female delinquency cases shot up 76 percent compared to a 42 percent increase for boys.*
- *The arrest rate for violent crimes almost doubled for girls.*
- *The arrest rate for property crimes went up 22 percent for girls while the boys' rate actually dropped.*

Sure, girls should be applauded for no longer taking on the role of the quiet wallflower that many of their ancestors did. Undoubtedly, girls who don't speak up when people are taking advantage of them lose out. But when female aggression becomes out-and-out criminal activity, there's cause for alarm.

The new millennium sees girls going through change and confusion. Should they take an aggressive stance with guys—asking them out, pushing for sex, paying for dates—or should they allow the guy to be the hunter in charge? While girls feel comfortable being more aggressive than they had been in the past, testosterone is and always will be the main source of energy for boys. It's the reason that boys fly off the handle instead of either crying or letting their emotions simmer. It's the reason boys feel the need to dominate their territory and even, perhaps, their girlfriends. It's the reason boys take up to seven hours longer than girls to process how they're feeling. It's the reason boys try to problem-solve and fix crisis situations as soon as they occur.

Despite their out-of-control hormones, boys need to feel that they are in control of their lives. But just because they make a case to have control, it does not always mean that it will satisfy them. Like any human being, boys want a challenge. Some guys just get off on the chase. They run after a girl, and when she finally declares her love for them, they are no longer interested. They want to work for a girl's affections, and win her heart as though she is a prized possession. The harder they have to work, the more they appreciate their prize. Although they may push a girl to give in to their desires, unless they really love her, many boys will quickly lose respect for her the moment they get what they want. I get too many letters from girls who learn that lesson only too late.

Playing Hard-to-Get

To make themselves seem less available and more terrific than they actually are, a lot of girls are taught to play hard to get. They make themselves scarce when their guy is trying to find them, they constantly tell him they're busy when they're really not. They act like they have loads of guys just drooling for them. Frankly, I don't like the idea of girls playing any games in an attempt to get a guy to love them. I believe that when we play games, we attract game-players who will only end up giving us back our own medicine. Would you be happy with a guy who purposely does not answer the phone to make you think he's out? Would you like to care for a guy who goes out of his way to make you jealous? Would you want to be involved with someone who rejects getting together with you just because you spontaneously called him at the last minute? Well if you answered no to any of these questions, put yourself in the shoes of a guy. Remember, we attract the same behaviors in a guy that we put forth.

So instead of *playing games*, girls should keep enjoying the activities they've always loved. If you're afraid that you will lose him to someone else, get this: nothing you do will keep him honest anyway. As I've said throughout this book, and as I will repeat more extensively later, the most important thing is your own sense of fulfillment.

Foolishly Putting Out for More

Linda was one of those girls who found out the hard way. She met Brad on Valentine's Day and really fell hard. She had sex with him the second time they met. Right after the act, he turned to her and said, "Linda, I really hope you didn't have sex with me thinking that I'm gonna ask you out. I like you and everything—but my mind is with Rachel. One day she's with her boyfriend, then the next day she says she wants to be with me. I really like her and I hope our relationship can work out." Linda didn't even have the good sense to get out of there. Instead, she got it on with him again the same night, thinking that she could change his mind. The next day when they were on-line together, they found that they really had nothing to talk about. Now whenever they see each other, each of them detours in another direction. All Linda says now is, "I can't believe Brad did that to me." Little did she know that she *let* him.

Guys are not that difficult to understand. They may appear as though they have it easy, and that they walk around without a care in the world, but keep in mind, they are pressured to feel they've got to prove their manhood. And if a girl *lets* them, they'll prove it with her. For a boy, it's a big responsibility to avoid being called a "wuss." They go out of their way to impress their buddies. They pressure girls for sex, they burp, fart, act loud, and behave like Neanderthals. *Yuck!* Many of them even go out of their way to appear insensitive and hide their soft side. Yet, despite all the show, guys still want the same thing girls do: love. They just have a different way of showing it, for fear they'll be ridiculed by their pals. Smart girls know that all their posturing is mucho macho stuff. A lot of times, girls have to be detectives to find out what guys *really* mean by some of their bizarre antics. But girls should also be careful not to let them get what they want just because they go heavy on the pressure. Remember that while Linda gave her body and her feelings to Brad, where was he? He was pining away for Rachel, who had been giving him a hard time!

Unfortunately, Linda is not the only girl who jumped into bed too soon.

Dear Dr. Gilda:

I have been going out with my boyfriend for about two months. I've already had sex with him, but now it seems that every time he comes over we have to have sex. I want a real relationship with him, but it seems like all he wants is sex. What should I do?   *Suffering*

Dear Suffering:

You can never unring the bell. In other words, I wish I had received this letter when you were merely *considering* having sex with him at such an early stage of your relationship. Teenage boys will take sex wherever they can get it; it's their hormonal urge. On the other hand, you probably wanted to please him early on, and maybe you thought you would be fulfilled as well. But you rushed into things much too quickly. So since you raised his level of expectation, he's expecting that level to continue indefinitely. Obviously, now you realize that this is not what you want.

Understand that your needs are the most important thing to fulfill. If you don't want to have sex, honor your body and refuse. If that means that your boyfriend gets mad and leaves, look at what you learned. Maybe we'll both be surprised and he'll tell you that he adores you for who you are and even if you don't have sex, he'll still be by your side. Frankly, you wrote me this note because you're worried that he won't go that route. So, if that's how it turns out, cut your losses, live with your mistakes, and vow to be wiser in your next encounter.

Dr. Gilda

Some girls just don't get it. Once a girl gives in to his pleading and begging, the challenge is gone, he's won his prey, and many guys are ready to move on. No one should jump into a sexual relationship before they know their partner for a long time.

When a girl has a strong inner self, she recognizes that the surges her guy is experiencing have more to do with the hormones inside his body than the feelings of caring he says he has for her. A girl with a strong inner self won't believe the "I love yous" that guys often utter just to get a free feel. Girls with sturdy inner selves do the things they love to do regardless of whether a guy is in their lives or not. Audrey, by saying that her boyfriend "means too much to me," places herself at his beck and call. No girl should devote her whole emotional life counting on a guy always being there for her. She should remain independent, enjoying a wealth of activities and friends who turn her on.

Understanding guys is a big component of having successful relationships with them. Do you think that Melany understands them sufficiently to give in to sleeping with her boyfriend?

Dear Dr. Gilda:

Hi! I'm 15 years old and on December 23rd, my boyfriend and I will be going out for three months. I have really fallen hard for him. I honestly know I love him and he has been telling me out of nowhere that he loves me, too. Well, my problem is that we both want sex bad. But I am scared he will tell everyone when we do have sex, and I will be labeled "easy" while he's called a "stud." What should I do? He's already promised me he wouldn't tell anyone. But a guy's a guy, and I know they all can't help but tell that they had sex. Please answer me ASAP. Thank you very much!

Melany

Dear Melany:

I'm so glad you wrote to me before you did something you'd regret later. A guy who really loves his girlfriend will not be interested in bragging at her expense. Instead, he'll respect her and her reputation. I suggest that before you decide to actually get sexually involved, you get to know him a while longer so that you can feel absolutely sure that you can trust him. Waiting won't kill you, but feeling awful about people chattering about you behind your back might make you feel pretty bad. Try trusting him with a juicy secret, and see where he goes with that. It's better to be sure than sorry.

Dr. Gilda

Unlike a lot of girls I hear from who have sex and are sorry later, at least Melany is thinking about the consequences of her actions before she acts. It's always a good idea to check out what a guy is really feeling before you believe the words you want to believe.

Dear Dr. Gilda:

My boyfriend and I have been going out for four months. He says he likes me, and loves me, but I haven't seen him for three weeks. He says it's because of his busy schedule. His parents are split up so he has to make time for them. He is also in drama and runs track and cross-country. Do you think he does really like me, or do you think he's just using his activities as a reason not to see me, so he can cheat on me behind my back?

Vicki

Dear Vicki:

First of all, you shouldn't be with a guy you can't trust. Second, it's good that this guy has so many interests, because that's what makes him interesting. A guy who really wants to see a girl makes time for her, no matter what. However, if he uses the excuse of being "too busy," that's your cue to take care of yourself and find someone more emotionally available.   *Dr. Gilda*

When two people understand each other, they can form a friendship based on respect, which can even expand to love. Respect is the basis for listening and communicating, but it takes time to unfold. Without respect, no relationship can survive. Understanding where a guy is coming from is particularly important for girls because guys won't usually demonstrate or say much about their feelings. Girls' feelings get hurt if they have read more into a guy's words than they should have.

Guys tend to focus on performing tasks and goals rather than cultivating their sensitive side. It's a rare guy who will want to just hang out and hug his girlfriend. If anything, the guy usually wants to complete his goal of having sex. But girls want to bond—as in, have a relationship. As a guy's frustration mounts, he may begin to pressure his girlfriend to have sex with him. Many girls give in, not because they want the sexual act, but because they want to feel wanted, loved, and cherished. They want to be hugged, held, and told sweet words. And they fear that if they say no to their boyfriend, he'll get it somewhere else and leave them. Having sex for fear you'll be dumped is no reason to put out. Unfortunately, I receive too many letters from girls who have given in to their boyfriends' desires, only to be sorry later. But I've also received letters from girls who did not give in, and ended up sorry:

Dear Dr. Gilda:

Hi! I love your Web page. I'm 18 years old. Six months ago I began dating a 23-year-old boy. Everything was going great. He showed me his love, I met his family, and I thought all was fine. He is a person who always wants to be in pubs, discos, and at parties till late at night. I didn't have a problem with any of that. Every time he invited me someplace I went with him.

After six months, our relationship changed. He didn't call me as often, but he still took me out and it appeared that he still loved me.

One day, he talked to me and said he needed time because he was confused and he didn't know if he loved me as a friend or as a girlfriend. We were both crying. With great pain we made a promise to each other: I gave him time to decide what he wanted and he said he would call me for a decision.

Two months passed and I didn't see or hear from him. I was worried because I hoped we would be together again. Then my best friend ran into him. She asked him why he hadn't called me. He told her he was embarrassed to tell me that his mother had thrown him out of his house because he made his ex-girlfriend pregnant, and now he has to get married. I couldn't imagine that he could do that to me.

He finally came to my house and talked to me and told me he loved this other girl. I didn't understand that because I thought he loved me. We are supposed to be friends now, but he told me that he couldn't call or visit me because he was married. I understand that.

I am writing to you because I only think all this is my fault because I didn't go to bed with him. That's why he probably made that other girl pregnant. I don't know what to do without him. I really loved him and I still do.

Please help me. Please give me advice about how I

can go on with my life knowing that I will never have him again. I don't want to become sick because of this problem. I can't go on with my life. I want to be happy again, but just knowing that he is with another woman tears my heart out. I hope you can help me.   *Elissa*

Dear Elissa:

My dear, dear girl. This is not your fault at all. This guy is master of his own fate, and he chose to sleep with someone else even though he made those empty promises to you. When a guy loves a girl, he respects her and supports her wishes. He doesn't run out and make another girl pregnant. In fact, if he really loved this other girl, he would have been man enough to be more responsible and use a condom. Actually, it's a good thing you did not choose to have sex with him because if he had been sleeping with other girls and with you, too, all without protection, who knows what kind of diseases he could have given you. And that's not even to mention the fact that he could have made you pregnant, also. How would you have handled that? Nice guy he is!!

It seems that the universe has protected you by giving this dude to someone else. Of course, your feelings are hurt because you wonder how you could have been such a fool to fall for his lines. I hear from women much older than you who have made the mistake of giving into a guy's demands, only to be left with disease *and* a baby!

Women tend to blame themselves because we think relationships are our job to keep track of. That's simply not true. This guy cheated on you and there is no excuse for that. He lied to you. He allowed you to care for him without being honest. Ohhh, are you ever lucky!!

Be without a guy for a while so you can get yourself together. Believe me, you will recover from this and then you'll be sooo thankful. We've all been there. But this is how we learn to choose more wisely next time around. I am here for you. Please let me know how you're doing.   *Dr. Gilda*

Dear Dr. Gilda:

I am writing to thank you very much. I really needed to hear some words from a professional like you. I will try to go on and you bet I am not going to be with another guy for a while. I realize I need time for me. If there is no problem with this, I will continue writing to you to let you know how I am doing.

Again, thank you. I didn't know that there would be someone like you who is so interested in helping teenagers the way you have helped me.   *Elissa*

Girls have to understand what motivates guys, even those in their 20s and older, and they have to know exactly what they are willing to accept. This is where their boundaries come into play. Once they know their boundaries, girls must be willing to communicate their wants, and gracefully say no when an offer is not the same as what they themselves have in mind. Girls who have well-defined boundaries don't allow themselves to become pressured into doing something they're not comfortable with. It's a matter of respect, and it begins with a girl's respect for herself.

The Respect-Connect

Just as girls should demand respect from guys, it is also important to respect them back. Like the differences in our hormones, brains, and bodies, our two genders want respect in different ways. Girls want to be cherished and appreciated by their guys as giving, caring, attractive people. On the other hand, guys want respect from girls for excelling at an activity they perform—at school, sports, or a competition. Guys enjoy having their girlfriends watch them win a tennis championship or a basketball game. They crave their girl-friends' praise for having negotiated a great raise at work. They love it when their girlfriend makes a big deal when they ace a tough test. In other words, as much as we make fun of those sappy fairy tales, guys today still want to feel like heroes in the eyes of their ladies.

How Do I Communicate with My Guy?

Heroes are one thing, but the down-and-dirty stuff that really makes a relationship work involves honest and truthful communication. As with respect, honesty has to work both ways. Girls who want a cool guy, yet lie to the one they've got, eventually get what they deserve. Sharon, for example, is really setting herself up for a fall:

Dear Dr. Gilda:

My new boyfriend thinks that I'm older than I really am. I don't know how to tell him the truth. I'm 16, and he's five years older than I am. I'm afraid that if he finds out, he'll get really mad. We haven't been going out long, but I really need some advice to tell him the truth without having him hate me. What should I do? I need help!!!!
Sharon

Dear Sharon:

This is an easy problem to solve. Open your mouth, look your guy in the eyes, and say these words, "I'm sorry, but I'm younger than you think I am. I'm 16, not 19." If your boyfriend is angry that you lied to him, that would be understandable. No relationship can last if it's built on lies. Whether they're little white lies, or big, killer fibs, if you're going to have any kind of a future together, how can you develop trust if you think your partner isn't telling you the truth? Besides, put yourself in your boyfriend's shoes. How would you like to be the one who's the receiver of the lie?

The quicker you level with him, the better. And it's best that you do it yourself before he hears the truth from a third party. Since every action has a consequence, it's time you faced up to yours. If your guy values honesty a lot, this could be the end of your relationship. Or, he may be kind enough to be willing to give you a second chance. Whatever he chooses to do will show you the kind of character he has. Maybe you'll be able to beg for his forgiveness, and he'll allow it to blow over. But whatever you do, do it now.

Dr. Gilda

You must be honest with your guy so that when it is your turn to receive, you'll get honesty back. Otherwise, you'll be setting yourself up for lots of dishonest relationships in the future. Remember that:

Gilda Gram   What goes around comes around.

Good relationships require not only honesty, but sharing your feelings and being sensitive and vulnerable. I know, guys are not as apt to spill their guts the way girls are. Guys would rather not display their weak spots in front of the girls they like. Neither are they blabbers in the sense that you are. They will never replace the girlfriends you have that you can stay on the phone with for hours at a time. Even if they start out that way with you, once the romance is an accepted one, eventually you'll find that they'd rather join sporting events or hang with their friends than talk to you about touchy-feely things for hours on the phone. Smart girls don't take these behaviors personally. They just accept them as the way guys are.

Since guys are not that interested in communicating their feelings and talking about your relationship, it is up to you to show him how you want him to communicate with you. In other words, if a girl doesn't show him, a guy won't have a clue about how to speak to her about the things that are important in his life. Remember, cavemen didn't exactly come back to the cave to woo and coo to their women. In order to open this leveling process, girls must tell their boyfriends what style of communication they prefer, as well as when their boyfriend has missed the mark.

For example, if your guy is suddenly acting distant with you, before you accuse him of running around behind your back, make him feel safe and comfortable enough to open up to you about what's bugging him. Understand that this is difficult for him because he never wants to appear as though he's "less than a man" in your eyes. Recognize that he won't be open with you unless he's certain that you won't tease him about his sensitivity, that you won't make fun of him, and that you won't gossip about his personal problems to your friends. This sort of trust takes time, and he'll need to be very certain that he can trust you with his special information.

Maggie saw that Barry was beginning to withdraw more and more from their relationship. She was certain that there was no one else he was interested in. But she couldn't get him to tell her what was on his mind. Finally, in a lot of pain herself, she blurted out that she was having a particular family problem that she had been keeping private from even her closest friends. Her father was an alcoholic, and after some horrible and tumultuous fights with her mother over the course of about three years, they were finally getting divorced. This was ripping Maggie apart. She felt so close to Barry that she confided this to him.

The nice thing about venting your spleen is that once you do, your listener feels closer to you. That's because:

Gilda Gram   When you trust a guy with a secret, he is likely to trust you back with one of his.

After Maggie told Barry about her private ordeal, he felt much closer to her. She quickly felt the difference in the way they began opening up to each other. Until then, Maggie felt that their six-month relationship was pretty tight. But crises can either bring a couple closer together or rip them apart. Once Maggie opened up to him, Barry then revealed that his own mom and dad were also getting divorced. Now he confided that he was glad he had someone to share his grief with. Actually, their mutual problems brought this couple closer together because:

What's the best way to have good communication? Declare your expectations in one clear statement. That means no ranting and raving or lengthy criticism about his not calling when he says he will. Guys are very sensitive to a woman's judgments, and you don't want him to wonder if he's really speaking to his critical mother. If he feels put down in any way, he'll retreat to his safety net of *not* communicating at all, as Lindsay is experiencing with her boyfriend:

Dear Dr. Gilda:

I am 17, and I have had a boyfriend now for over four months. Things were absolutely great in the beginning, never a dull moment or a dull conversation. But now it seems that every time we speak on the phone, we have trouble saying things to each other. Hanging out with him and seeing him in school is amazing, and I love it. I don't know how to, I guess you can say, "rekindle" what we had. And I have to do it soon before I lose him. He decided to work at the same camp as me during the summer. That's not making me happy either.

Lindsay

Dear Lindsay:

It is possible that you're very attracted to each other physically, so when you are face-to-face, the firecrackers continue to blast off. But when you are on the phone, that's when you may discover that you really don't share a lot in common. Maybe you're at the point of becoming bored with each other, since you said that you're not thrilled that he will be working with you during the summer. Or maybe he's so accepted your relationship that he's ready to move back to spending more time with the guys.

Even though you're not excited that he'll be at your summer camp, you say that you don't want to lose him. What's that about? Girl, what exactly is it that you do want? You should determine this before the summer begins so that you can either go to camp as a couple, or go as platonic friends.

Gilda Gram

The fear of losing a guy should never be the reason for holding on to him.

At first, most relationships begin as hot romances. But what really sustains a good relationship over time is the ability of two people to share their experiences and feelings. If you're having problems after only four months, it's time to reassess what's really happening.

Is it possible that your guy no longer feels safe sharing his feelings with you? Maybe without knowing it, you hurt him with some careless remarks. Remember, guys are very sensitive about being criticized. The only way you'll find this out is to ask him openly and make him feel comfortable enough to level with you.

But still and all, you must determine what it is you want. Once you determine that, if you decide to close the door on this guy, a better door will eventually open with someone better for you. But you must have the courage to sense that the communication problem you're having after just this short amount of time is telling you something about the future of the two of you. Open your eyes and see the writing on the wall before you find yourself involved in a summer of regret.   *Dr. Gilda*

So the way to be honest and open in your communication is to offer your guy a simple, short, "I need you to call when you promise you will" to let him know what you expect from him. Without telling him your strategy, you've shared your boundaries. Now let the issue go.

Real communication with guys is usually hard to come by, especially at the beginning of a relationship. Trust has not yet been established, and as much as girls would like to blame guys for not being as open as they are, at the beginning of a relationship neither one of you is entirely comfortable spilling your guts. Although most teens prefer instant gratification, good relationships take time to build. Since girls are usually better communicators than guys, here are eight tips you can follow to get your guy to open his sensitive side.

8 Tips to Pry the Often-Shy

1. Since guys generally don't feel comfortable sharing their feelings, especially at the beginning of a relationship, ask your guy what he *thinks* about something instead of what he *feels* about it. Even then, you don't want to ask a general "What are you thinking?" question. He'll interpret that to mean that you want to know what he's thinking about *you*, and he will probably be unwilling to fess up—because that's really what he's *feeling*! So be sure to specify your question to limit the confusion.

2. Since guys are goal-driven, encourage him to describe what he *did*, rather than how he *felt*. If you can get him to *describe* and boast about what he did, and then *listen to him carefully, with enthusiasm*, he'll get the impression that you really care. A guy who is convinced his girlfriend cares will be more apt to discuss his feelings that go deeper than, say, how psyched he was about fixing his dirt bike. *What a guy!*

3. If you want to find out his views on love, after you have seen a movie or TV show together, or after you have both observed the break-up of mutual friends, get him to express his thoughts—which will lead to his feelings—about the situation. That will lead to his sharing his own take on love and relationships in general. You can learn a lot from a guy when you use someone else as the subject.

4. Since guys are not as talkative as you and your friends are, ask open-ended questions that begin with "How?" and "Why?" If you avoid questions that require only a one-word response, your guy will be more likely to expand on what he starts to say.

5. Since guys have the rep for being such poor listeners, welcome him to chime in with his opinions while you're speaking to him.

6. Don't ever think that your guy friends can substitute for your girlfriends when it comes to detailed communication. Girls usually like to blab with intricate information far more than boys. Even if you have a guy you adore, by keeping girlfriends around you ensure that you'll get the kind of communication feedback you need without pressuring your guy to give you something about which he doesn't feel comfortable.

7. Decode what he's really saying. It's tough for a guy to honestly tell you he loves you. Instead, he'll criticize the dorky boy who always hangs out at your locker. Or he'll tell you that the gorgeous hunk you laugh with in geometry is not so cute after all. Although he's not saying it in exactly the words you'd like, his green-eyed monster is telling you something his words are neglecting.

8. Most important, let him know you can keep his personal information and even the cutesy romantic stuff you share just between the two of you. Remember his need to be a "guy's guy" and keep the image of macho man. He'll be humiliated if he hears that your girlfriends know his secrets, and he'll be mortified if the guys get wind of his vulnerable

side. If you blow his cover even once, he'll never trust you again, and it will be curtains for the relationship.

Since we spend a lot of time talking, we all believe we know how to communicate. When you follow these eight steps, you're on your way to getting your guy to at least begin communicating more openly. But the reality is that being a good communicator takes practice. It starts with feeling comfortable with the person you're talking to. Before you fool yourself into thinking that you have what it takes to communicate well yourself with your special someone, complete the Comfortable Communication Quiz and see where your one-on-ones are headed:

COMFORTABLE COMMUNICATION QUIZ

Beside each question, write Yes or No.

_____ 1. Do I communicate with my guy like he's one of my buds?

_____ 2. Do I know about his family?

_____ 3. Can I act silly or stupid when I'm with him without feeling self-conscious?

_____ 4. Do I know what he's interested in?

_____ 5. Do I know what makes him laugh?

_____ 6. Do I know what makes him sad?

_____ 7. Do I freely share my feelings with him?

—— 8. Do I feel "safe" communicating with him, knowing that he won't tease or embarrass me?

Score Card

1–3 Yes : You're like strangers now, and you need to get to know each other much better before you believe you're an item.

4–5 Yes : As well as you think you know each other, you still need to become more comfortable and open.

6–8 Yes : You've got the makings of a rosy future. Whatever you're doing, keep it up.

Karlie took the Comfortable Communication Quiz and found that she scored 4 yeses. When we started to talk about her score, she admitted that she still needed to feel "safe" around her boyfriend of three months. It seems that he continued to embarrass her with her friends, which made her feel uncomfortable. When I asked her to describe an embarrassing event, she told me this story:

Brad is super great to me, and sweet and everything. I truly love him with all my heart, and he knows it. But he's been frustrating me lately because he always asks for my friends' screen names, and when I give them to him he goes straight to his e-mail and cusses them out. He knows that I wouldn't leave him for anything in the world, so he doesn't care what he does. I told him to stop doing that to people because they all think bad of him. He's not a bad guy at all, but he won't leave my friends alone. Now most of my friends hate him! I don't want to leave him for good, but I'm wondering if backing off for a while might help him realize that I'm REALLY sick of it.

I explained to Karlie that respect for her wishes is a very important trait of a cool boyfriend. Although she thinks Brad is "super great" to her, "sweet and everything," she's really in another world. In reality, he has dissed her wishes. I also told her that I was concerned that she couldn't say no to him when he asked her to give him the screen names of her friends. I told her, "If you can't say no to Brad for a small request like this, what will happen when he asks you to do something you find really objectionable? The cost of your unwillingness to say no may prove too great," I told her. Learn to exercise your inner self on little things so when the bigger issues arise, they'll be no problem for you to handle.

I went on to explain that this example shows how she must decide what she wants, she must be willing to speak her mind, and she must decide what she's prepared to do if her wishes are trashed by Brad. As long as she's not totally honest with him about her feelings, she will be playing the role of someone else, saying things that are not coming from her own heart. As a result, she'll never feel safe communicating with this dude.

Taking this Comfortable Communication Quiz was Karlie's wake-up call to herself that if Brad was not respecting her wishes, she had to abandon her silly vow never to leave him. She knew that she had an obligation to respect herself. Finally, she admitted that respect would begin after she reconsidered the kind of caring she was NOT getting. She knew she had to begin by learning to say no.

Saying No Can Make You Feel Good

Saying no is a difficult chore for most females, young and old. Being the nurturers that we are, we don't want our friends to feel bad, we don't want to gain enemies, we want to be liked, and we don't want to ruin the relationships that mean so much to us. Even though this belief is not true, we mistakenly think it's our feminine obligation to keep the peace. So as a result, in an effort to make nice, we lie about being willing to do something or want something, and we say yes when we really want to say no. In short, many of us are people pleasers not just with guys, but with everyone we meet. In the end, we give away a part of ourselves by not being totally frank. Then we become angry, upset, and stressed that we have allowed ourselves to be pushed to the limit. Usually, though, we don't become angry with the right person. Instead of being angry with ourselves for agreeing to something we didn't really want to agree to from the start, we become angry with our parents, our friends, our boyfriends, or whoever made the original offer. Keep in mind:

Gilda Gram   We are responsible for our own actions.

It also pays to remember that every action we take has a consequence of some kind. So, the first pact girls must make with themselves is:

Gilda Gram   I agree not to go along to get along.

It is not a good enough reason to lie to yourself or to accept shabby treatment just to get along with a particular "in" crowd. Consider standing on your own for a while. Breathe in the free air and realize how terrific it is not to have to answer to people whose values you don't share. Say, "Ahhhhh." Being free of someone else's restrictions is worth more than anything else in the world. Just ask anyone who has been in jail!

The second insight girls must recognize is:

Gilda Gram   If a guy doesn't respect my wishes, he doesn't care about me.

It may be tough to accept that you have to dump a guy because he's not on your side. But it's better that you find this out sooner rather than later, after you've invested a lot of feelings over a longer period of time. If anything, once you discover that he's gotta go, thank the universe that you came to your senses as soon as you did. Then be prepared to move on. Life has a funny way of rewarding us for making the right decisions. After you've dumped the guy who's been giving you so much grief, watch who comes strolling your way. It's undoubtedly some *new* dude who's cooler than cool. As soon as you meet him, you'll wonder what you ever saw in your old crush.

How would you respond to this scenario? Steve's parents are going to be away for the weekend, and Steve has planned a big bash at his house while they're gone. You know Steve's friends are part of the faster crowd at school, and you also know that your parents would kill you if they found out that you went to a party where there would be drugs, sex, and alcohol. They've grounded you in the past for far less horrific things, and you're sure you would not be allowed out for three months if caught. You're crazy about Steve and you are so glad he finally asked you out. He's begging you to go to his shindig. How do you handle the clash of your parents' values and Steve's?

We've all wanted to be at somewhere that, for some reason, we couldn't attend. It surely makes us feel bad that we're missing all the fun while it seems that everyone else is having a blast. If this happens to you, you feel like an outcast, as if you've been excluded from the most important event of the century. Maybe you can't go to a basketball game because you have to study for a final exam in a subject that has you sweating. Maybe you can't go to a major party because this is the weekend that you spend with your father who doesn't live with you. Maybe you've been grounded for being caught at a friend's house after you lied to your mom and told her you were at the library. Whatever the reason, when you can't go to an event that you've been dying to go to, of course you feel bummed.

Okay, so it's a fact of life that you will have to decline Steve's invitation. But how do you do it in a way that will communicate that you are interested in him, and that you'd like him to invite you next time around?

First of all, understand that there are ways of saying no and feeling good. Study the following surefire strategies on:

5 Steps to Turning Him Down Without Turning Him Off

1. Remind yourself that you not only have the right to say no, but you have an obligation to be true to yourself and your own values. Sure, as a teenager, your values may be those forced on you by your parents, but ultimately you're the one who will suffer the consequences if your folks find out that you lied to them.

2. Offer a *very* short and simple explanation for why you can't go, and suggest an alternative plan to get together. This way your Steve won't take it personally, believing you think he's some dork you're not interested in. For example, say, "Steve, I'd love to go to your party, but my folks will ground me for life if they find out that your parents are not going to be home. Instead, can we get together after school tomorrow?" This way you may be turning him down, but not letting him down.

3. Be sure not to be drawn into your crush's pleading or emotional blackmail. Any guy who pressures you to change your mind with statements like, "Your parents will never find out" or "If you don't come to the party, I'll have to find

another date" does not have your best interests at heart. All he's really saying is that he cares solely about his own desires, and he demands you to do whatever it takes to satisfy them. This kind of guy doesn't want a girlfriend. He needs a pacifier!

Dear Dr. Gilda:

Why are men such babies?   *Elizabeth*

Dear Elizabeth:

Men are such babies because we women baby them!

Dr. Gilda

Gilda Gram

If a guy you turn down threatens to find someone else, tell him to go ahead. Then you go ahead, too—to a new guy. *Next!*

---

4. Use the 3 Bes: *Be* brief. *Be* friendly. *Be* firm. If you even hint that you're wishy-washy about changing your mind, your guy will use that as leverage and do everything he can to change it for you. Follow the 3 Bes, but as you do, disengage your eye contact, turn your body away from him, and change the subject. From these cues, he will learn that the case is permanently closed.

5. If it's still tough for you to say no, especially to a guy you're crushing on, buy some time. Time-buying is easy if you use one of these statements:

"I don't think my folks will let me, but I'll ask them anyway. Let me see what I can do."

Or,

"I have to study now. Let's talk about it later."

Or,

"Let's see, the party's not until next Friday. I have a week to work on my parents."

Gilda Gram   Time-buying techniques take the pressure off you while you decide how you want to proceed.

At first, if you're not used to it, saying no to people you'd rather say yes to will be a challenge. You'll find that some of your friends will not want to accept the word readily. Or, no matter what you do, still others may take your rejection personally and call you a "bitch." No matter how other people react, remember your strong inner self. Remember that it's only you who will have to live with the consequences of your actions. Make your decision and stick to your guns!

After you've mastered these principles, you'll begin to feel better about yourself and your ability to communicate your boundaries. Communicating your boundaries will show others how much respect you have for yourself.

Whenever I get a letter like the following, I feel good that there are girls out there who have truly spent the time sharpening their inner self:

Dear Dr. Gilda:

I need some help. I just broke up with my boyfriend. He's calling me very bad names (slut, for example). I'm really fed up with it. He's not taking the break-up well. How can I tell him that I'm sick and tired of his attitude and I can't handle it anymore without lowering myself to his level? I don't want to be mean or nasty the way he is. I just want to be very straightforward about how I feel. Do you have any advice?

Sincerely,
Jill

Dear Jill:

It's wonderful to hear from such a mature young woman. You're right to feel that you don't want to get down to your boyfriend's level—no way, no how, not now! If he's rolling in mud, let him roll there alone.

Apparently, this guy believed that you would accept his poor treatment of you indefinitely. That's why he can't believe you gave him the heave-ho, and why he's hurting so bad now. That's just tough! I'm sure you gave him plenty of warnings before you pulled the plug for the last time.

Use the "S&S" approach to let him know you mean business: make your comments Short & Sweet. After you've delivered your message, change the subject or walk away. He'll quickly get it that his begging and pleading will do him no good if they go on deaf ears. Maybe next time he'll understand that people who choose to hang out with him deserve to be cherished rather than dissed! Whatever you do, keep reminding yourself that:

Gilda Gram
There's a lot of love in saying no.

The kind of love in the word *no* is the level of respect you have for yourself. Go for it, girl. I applaud you.   *Dr. Gilda*

When you demonstrate that you care about yourself, others will know that you can care about them.

Gilda Gram
When you can say—and mean—"I love *me*" you'll be able to say—and mean—"I love *you*" to a guy.

If these are the standards you follow, it won't be long before you decide you want to find guys who are strong in spirit like you. These are the guys who become cool boyfriends.

All people go through good days and bad days, with lots of ups and downs. Teenagers probably have more drastic highs and lows than adults because this is the time in their lives when their hormones take a roller-coaster ride. Understanding these hormonal spurts makes it easier to forgive bizarre behavior. But there is no excuse for putting up with treatment that is anything less than respectful. Love is terrific, but it doesn't mean that someone you care about has the right to take advantage of you. To protect yourself against anything but the best treatment from both your friends and your guys:

1. Know what you want.
2. Establish your boundaries.
3. Communicate your boundaries.
4. Be committed to accepting only the very best treatment.
5. Be prepared to walk away if you don't get the respect you want.

A worthy guy shows you he's terrific because he demonstrates 3 Cs:

1. Character
2. Compassion
3. Commitment

With Character, he has a backbone so he can stand up to even his goofy friends when they tell him he's acting too mushy with you. With Compassion, he's not afraid to show how much he cares. With Commitment, you'll know that you can depend on him to be there for you, and trust him to be honest and open.

Above all, every girl should know:

Gilda Gram   You deserve to be honored and adored.

NEED #3

Create Your Own Excitement

Someone once told us that, in matters of the heart, two halves make a whole. So for centuries, we've mistakenly believed that each of us has a "missing piece" in the form of someone out there who will round out our edges and provide the stuff that we ourselves lack. It's a continuation of the fairy tales that taught young women that "someday my prince will come," and *he'll* be our savior who will make us better than we actually are. What about us being our own savior? *Helloooo . . .*

For many years, the entertainment industry created movies and TV shows with adventurous male heroes. They knew that male viewers would watch males and female viewers would watch males. But things are different these days. Teenage girls now seem to have their own TV network in the WB. One of the network's most popular series is *Buffy the Vampire Slayer,* with its star a teenage girl who, like the Lone Ranger, single-handedly rescues humanity from evil. So teen girls do have role models that show that they can act and live independently, without the aid of some guy. If this is the case, why does the story seem to change as soon as a girl wants love?

Girls think that they are not capable, kind, funny, beautiful, or intelligent on their own. They think that an all-powerful guy will get them to transform from ugly duckling into beautiful swan. They also believe that he will remove their feelings of emptiness and low self-esteem. In the movie *Jerry McGuire,* one of the main characters revealed to the other, "You complete me." I hear many teenage girls confess that they're scared to be alone, and they *need*—mind you, *need*—a boyfriend to fill their loneliness and make them feel that they are pretty.

While the idea of completion is fun to explore, and Hollywood has certainly made it seem desirable, in the real world, it's doubtful that half a person will ever find happiness. That would make her only half of what she can be. Since people attract people like themselves, you can bet that half a person will attract nothing more than a half-witted counterpart!

That is not to say that people don't unconsciously look for mates with opposite traits. As we all know, opposites do attract. But anyone who has ever been in a relationship will tell you that while opposites attract, if they're not the right *kind* of opposites, over time they repel. For example, a person with a lively and outspoken personality will attract a more quiet mate for obvious reasons. Imagine two big-mouths trying to hook up! They'd always be competing for the podium as each vies for attention to speak. So of course, a lively girl would seek out a quieter guy, and vice versa.

In contrast to the more superficial personality traits, character traits lie deep beneath the surface. In the real world, beyond the fictitious romances portrayed on the big and small screens, people who make it as a couple have to agree on what's important to them beyond the superficial gloss. What are your likes? What makes you happy? What are your goals? These have nothing to do with your cute crush donning the coolest clothes or having the greatest smile. Those traits wear thin very quickly. No, values and beliefs go much deeper, and because they're so deep, when they're well matched they form a bond that lasts.

For example, if your crush values smoking weed and you don't, he may pressure you to conform to his values, believing that you're too square the way you are. Meanwhile, you may begin pressuring him to stop smoking weed, as you feel a pang of disrespect for him. No matter what the other person does, the pressures that each will put on the other to conform can derail a relationship. Sizing up even the obvious personality differences between you can take time, so learning each other's hidden character traits should not be taken lightly—another good reason to wait a while before jumping into commitment.

Dear Dr. Gilda:

I have been with my boyfriend for five months. He's real good-looking and he's got a great body. But now I'm fed up with his sloppy eating habits. Whenever we go to a restaurant, food always drips down his face and onto his clothes. It's embarrassing! I really thought I loved him, but now I'm not so sure. What should I do?

Alicia, 15 years old

Dear Alicia:

This is exactly the reason why you must get to know a guy well before you commit yourself to love him. Although you are apparently a neater eater than your guy, and this is only a superficial difference, the eating behaviors he is exhibiting are really starting to gnaw at you. And it's only been five months into the relationship! Imagine what would happen if you were together for a year.

It's a good thing that you are getting to know him in a lot of different situations. Remember the Make-a-Choice Quiz? Return to that Quiz, and see if you really want to continue keeping your guy around. Remember that what bugs you about his behavior may be perfectly all right with another girl. But keep in mind that *your* feelings are your feelings and you're entitled to them. If you find that his eating is too disgusting, you may want to tell him that you'd prefer that he become neater when the two of you are eating out. Or, you may decide to pack him in altogether. Finding out about different traits of different people is what going out with a variety of guys is about:

> **Gilda Gram**   Dating is practice for the future.

Once you decide either to quit being "embarrassed" by your guy's sloppy behavior and accept him as he is, or that you no longer want to put up with his poor eating habits, you'll know exactly how to proceed next.

Dr. Gilda

The Benefit to Getting Whole

So now that you know that two halves do NOT make a whole relationship, it's wise to consider becoming a complete human being—a finished product—on your own, before you even consider hooking up with a mate. All you girls out there who think you're fab only when you have a guy had better listen up. You'd better get complete on your own because if you're depending on a guy to complete you, remember, he's got his own problems, and he doesn't need yours.

> **Gilda Gram**   A boyfriend doesn't make you happy. YOU make you happy.

Of course, if you already have a boyfriend, it's never too late to start taking care of yourself. If you're in a relationship that is too demanding, too controlling, too restricting, if you've changed yourself so much to please your guy that you hardly even recognize who you are when you look in the mirror, the time has come to get wise and get strong. What do *you* want to do? If you don't do what you want, you're being dishonest. If you're being dishonest, you're attracting someone who's settling for less of a girl. That's not a cool guy. The better you are, the more a guy who's cool will want you. But:

Gilda Gram   You must start doing the work on yourself alone.

Of course, as a teenager, you're still developing, and so it would be impossible to become the person you will be in say, ten years. And that's fine. But what you must do—and this is what I mean by suggesting that you become "whole"—is to continue to enjoy the activities you love, continue to have an active social life with your friends, continue to plug away at your school work, continue to strive to be an It Girl—whether you already have a boyfriend or not. These are the qualities that make you whole at this age, and, in fact, at any age, and they also make you and your colorful life more interesting to a guy.

Gilda Gram   Being whole attracts the cool guys.

As you make an investment in yourself and you become a *really* hot chick, you'll find a mate who is similarly hot. (He might even turn out to be that formerly ungettable guy!) Together you can form a *partnership* where you discover new sides to each other. This definitely beats *hero worship*, with you crushing on him as he gets off on your adoration. On the other hand, if two of you meet when neither of you has developed your interests, you'll end up competing as you demand more and more from the other. Those demands will increase because you are both thinking of the other person as being in your life to fill your gaps. Terrible power struggles and arguments will occur over the smallest things. Instead, when two *partners* join forces, love does not become a push-and-pull struggle. The art of attracting a cool guy is that simple.

Get There by Being Home Alone

No matter how busy you are and how committed you want to be to your friends, schoolwork, job, family, or guy, it is essential that you schedule time for yourself. That may mean reserving time to just sit and gab on the phone or in a chat room. Or it may mean finding time to do absolutely nothing. This is the time when not one other person will interfere in your space and dictate what *their* rules are.

What are the benefits of chilling out? Plenty. Even in small doses, goofing off is essential to your health and happiness. Being alone provides you moments to dream your dreams. No one will come kicking down your door, telling you that you're not pretty enough, or thin enough, or smart enough to do what you dream to do. This is the time when if you want to believe that you're going to be the next class president, you'll be able to have that vision and devise a strategic plan. If you want to fantasize about becoming a famous recording artist, you'll be able to do that, too.

You don't have to just sit in your room. You can go to the beach, and spend hours watching the tide roll in. Or you can grab a glimpse of sunset, and imagine that the day's curtain is coming down. Or envision walking on a cloud, feeling the marshmallowy pillows on your toes, knowing that the sky is far below. Or listen to your favorite CD, or watch your best-loved TV program, or rent a video. Sing, dance, moan, groan. Take a nap. The time is yours to do with what you want.

Time alone is vital because it is your down time, the time you need to catch your breath. It's when you don't have to satisfy others, or put on a happy face, or dress to impress. With so few things in our life that *really* belong to us, this is *your* own time.

Just like one of your subjects at school, consider time alone as your special course in self-development. It might be a good idea to do a Best Bud Tune-up. In an earlier chapter, we discussed the traits of good friends. But when you're growing and maturing, your friendships change often, and you need to continue to reassess whether the friends you've got are doing you justice. Who are your best friends right now? Take your alone time to complete this quiz and decide whether all of them should be keepers:

BEST BUD TUNE-UP

Answer Yes or No to 1. and 2. below:

———— 1. Do my best buddies defend me and bend for me?

———— 2. Do they drain me and pain me?

Score Card

If you answered yes to Question 1, you've got good friends now, and you should continue to take this tune-up after you've established other new friend-ships. If you answered yes to Question 2, you need to do an overhaul and edit your friendship list. Be pre-pared to replace the friends you've got with new ones who care about you.

These kinds of questions can only be answered when you're quietly by yourself and you can really think about who's in your life. Certainly, you couldn't respond to these questions while you're out.

Another time-alone activity is to assess the studly guy you're gushing over. It's fine to have a crush, but is your cutie crushing back on you? There are lots of girls who have a serious interest in a guy, but they are so in awe of him, they never expose their own personalities. So ultimately, it's only about him! Part of caring for a boyfriend is letting him get to know you as much as you've gotten to know him. It's important that you both honestly open up to each other.

Have you done that? Take your time alone to find out if the deep feelings you have for him are two-sided or a one-way deal.

CRUSH-ON-YOU! QUIZ

Answer Yes or No to each of the following:

_____ 1. Does he remember your birthday and other important occasions?

_____ 2. Does he agree to accompany you to boring family outings?

_____ 3. Does he call you to say he misses you after you see him?

_____ 4. Does he stick to plans you've made together?

_____ 5. Does he give off obvious signs that he's over his ex?

_____ 6. Does he say nice things about you when you're not around?

_____ 7. Does he go out of his way to see you at school, at your job, or at your friends'?

Score Card

5–7 Yes : This cutie's crushing back big time!

3–4 Yes : Maybe he's missed the signs or maybe he needs more encouragement. There is definitely some interest there, but you'll have to do more fishing before you can reel this flounder in.

1–2 Yes : Give it up. You're experiencing hero worship, not partnership, and you know that if your feelings are not returned, it's time to find a better cutie to return your favors. Just as you were able to learn some things about yourself and your relationships when you were alone to do these quizzes, taking time out for yourself also gives you the opportunity to consider the sexual pressure you may be feeling from the guy who says he wants you bad. Or how to handle your very protective and overbearing parents. Or, how to devise better ways to earn more money. Or, how to handle your killer breakup. That's when you especially need time to chill on your own.

Breather After a Breakup

Ginny was devastated. She had just been dumped by Charlie, whom she had been seeing for two years. The breakup came as a big shock to her because Ginny thought things were fine between them. She even fantasized that some day they'd get married. About a year ago, he had bought her a beeper so he could reach her whenever he wanted. She abided by his request to have her call him every hour, and she gave in to his wishes whenever he wanted sex. She thought she was the ideal girlfriend and that he'd never leave. When he told her she couldn't hang out with her girlfriend Joan, she listened. When he told her to wear less makeup, she obeyed. When he screamed at her for wearing a skirt he thought was too short, she peeled it off. What Ginny didn't know is that she allowed Charlie to control her. She gave him her soul. At first, guys who control girls enjoy the power. But after the initial rush, it gets boring and old.

That's what happened to Charlie. Suddenly, without warning, he told the 17-year-old that he didn't want to have a steady girlfriend in his life anymore. He said he felt that he was missing out on a lot and he felt tied down. That was on a Friday. By Saturday he had already been spotted escorting a pretty and popular girl at their school to the movies. Ginny cried inconsolably for days.

But what might have been the worst *year* of her life instead turned into a short-lived mourning period because Ginny learned about the mistakes she had made. A mourning period is absolutely necessary after you lose someone, although some girls run from one romance to another without even a moment to consider what really went wrong. That's not a good idea. Just as every action has a consequence, every consequence has a lesson:

Gilda Gram   After a high or after a low, always ask, "What did I learn?"

Unless you figure out the mistakes you made, and even why you liked this guy, you're likely to repeat the same mistakes with the next guy you attract. Sure, he might look different, sound different, and be different from the guy you left behind, but mark my words, he'll have the same difficult qualities you had never learned to recognize and deal with in your past. Love is funny in that regard:

> **Gilda Gram**
> Relationships are less about finding love and more about learning about yourself.

Learning about yourself includes making mistakes, falling apart, learning your lessons, getting stronger and smarter, and moving on. This is growth. Being happy is part of growth, but so is having heartache. As much as I'd love to tell you otherwise, although the happy times are wonderful, we learn more about ourselves from our lows. And unfortunately, when it comes to being sad, there are no shortcuts to going through the pain:

> **Gilda Gram**
> The only way out of pain is to get through the pain. Feel the feelings so you can let them go.

To be able to let your feelings go, follow the 3-Step Take Care Plan:

3-Step Take Care Plan

1. *Get Busy.* Join the school paper, sign up for tennis lessons, volunteer at the local hospital. Do anything to take your mind off your breakup so you're just not waiting by the phone and feeling sorry for yourself.

2. *Get Solo.* Well, *some* amount of time feeling sorry for yourself is all right, just as long as you put a cap on how long you'll permit yourself to drown in your tears. Tell yourself,

"I'm giving myself one hour to cry. After that, I'm going to do my homework and study for that bio test I'm taking tomorrow." Instead of concentrating on your grief, focus on acing the test. Veg out, lounge in sweats with messy hair, and just think. Chant the feel-good mantra:

Gilda Gram   *For* a while, mope. *After* a while, cope.

3. *Get Friendly.* Good friends, the ones who passed the Best Bud Tune-up, will listen to you go on and on about the crush that crashed. Take some tips from Buffy, the Vampire Slayer. After her nights of passion with Angel ended in disaster, she found comfort by the side of her die-hard girlfriends instead of seeking other male attention. After your breakup, you'll probably be moaning about the same things again and again. Haven't you done the same for them when they were suffering a crisis? *Yeah, your breakup is a crisis!* Get down with your friends, strategize ways to feel better, review what went wrong in your relationship, and promise to go out with new-and-improved guys.

The important thing for girls to remember is not to repeat the same mistakes:

Gilda Gram   Let your *next* mistakes be *new* mistakes.

In order to be sure you don't repeat past errors, take some time to be alone. The problem is, lots of girls find spending time alone difficult after a breakup. They'd rather be surrounded by people who they think will help dull the pain. But in reality, although other people may be able to distract you temporarily, no one can dull the pain for you. You must always return home and be alone with your aching heart. If you schedule this time in advance, and understand the moping-then-coping approach to feeling better, you can prepare this time for yourself to map out the way you spend your next few weeks. You *will* feel better because you'll know that you're accomplishing things for yourself.

While you're alone, promise to do the following: whatever you do after your breakup, don't spend your precious time and energy conjuring up evil acts to get back at your ex. You may hate your guy because of the way he treated you. *And you're right!* You may vow never to lay eyes on him again. *And you're right!* You may promise yourself never to fall so hard for such a jerk. *And you're right!* But no matter what you do, remember:

Gilda Gram   Hate is not the opposite of love. Indifference is.

In other words, unless you are totally indifferent to what your ex is doing, what he's into, and who he's now dating, you're not over him, and you still need time to mend.

The amount of time it takes to heal is different for everyone. Sally Ann spent six months mourning the end of a one-year relationship, but Nettie needed only three weeks. To get totally over him and to accelerate your healing process, focus on *yourself*, not on him. Okay, it's human nature to feel that since you can't *have* him back, you'd love to *get* him back. Well, forget about it! Tripping his new girlfriend or flattening his tires or calling them and hanging up won't get you anywhere. All right, maybe you want to imagine him stepping in dog do with his best new shoes. That I'll allow you. But don't even think of stalking him and being a constant thorn in his side. (Besides, most states have laws against stalking, and your obsessiveness could actually land you in jail.) Also, don't even think about having sex with him to make him remember what he lost. Finally, perish the thought of trying to make him jealous, because you'll only make a fool of yourself when you find out he really doesn't care. Ultimately,

Gilda Gram   The best revenge is doing well.

Doing well involves getting into your own life and excelling at the things you love. Doesn't this sound familiar? Doesn't it sound like the habits of an It Girl? From the been-there, done-that school, the best It Girls have been down and out before they took control. Review the qualities of an It Girl. Strut your smarts as you devote passionate attention to the things you love, which will make you better at something you can use in the future.

How to Pump Up Your Passions

Interest*ing* chicks are interest*ed* chicks. This describes It Girls. It Girls pursue their passions. Passionate pursuers are a challenge to guys because while other girls may be chasing them, the It Girls are chasing their dreams. This makes it tough for the guys who are interested in them to get their attention. It's human nature—the things we have to work harder to get we value more. So if these It Girls are out pursuing their passions rather than pursuing the guys that others girls want, who do you think the guys will be interested in? Surely, not the easy ones! It's the ones who are hard to get who get their heart.

Notice I didn't say the ones who *play* hard to get. That's the difference between It Girls and girls whose main purpose is to snag a guy. It Girls are genuinely passionate about their activities and hobbies. Because their focus is not a guy, guys become curious about what these girls find so captivating. And passion is contagious. That's what makes It Girls so attractive to the opposite sex. They are so devoted to their dreams that they shine. Now *that's* attractive.

Completing a Passion Contract

Take a moment to assess what turns *you* on. (If you say, "nothing except a guy," you're in deep trouble.) This means you must discover what you love most about life. Then respond to the following:

1. What (I didn't say *Who*) have you been passionate about lately?

2. Name an activity you used to love, but with which you've lost touch.

3. When and why did you discard it from your schedule?

4. List a date when you'll restart it.

5. You've set a goal in motion. How does that make you feel?

Rekindling your passion gives you an instant attitude adjustment because you're doing something special for yourself. Now continue the exercise:

1. List your omigod-I-can't faults:

2. List your thank-you-very-much best qualities:

Which list was longer? Most girls say the first. It's easier to name your negatives than your positives because our society doesn't think it's cool to brag. But knocking yourself down won't give you the positive attitude you need. To succeed at your passions, tear down your personal fears about what others think. Up your energy. Boost your mood. Kick up your confidence. It's time to bask in your glory.

Now make yourself available and flirtable as you stand tall, raise your chin, uncross your arms, smile, and act approachable. You may elect to get a new hairstyle, a new outfit, or different makeup. But be careful that your motive for the new-and-improved you is *not to try to reclaim your ex*, but to *make yourself feel fresher and better*. You are the only one who counts now. If this guy really cared for you he'd still be in your life.

Once you're on the right path you'll feel it. And then one day out of the blue a friend will mention Joe's name. Without a moment's hesitation, you'll reply, "Huh? Joe who?" Your own response might even surprise you, but you'll know this dude is history once and for all.

Finding Guys on the Internet

In this age of high tech, I am meeting more and more people who have found true love on the Internet. Getting to know someone well before you meet face-to-face is one way to prevent physical *dis*traction. This could be an especially good method for meeting guys if a girl is shy. Many girls feel safe about sharing personal information with a perfect stranger, realizing that the stranger could never jump through the computer screen and hurt them. So they open up about themselves quickly, unlike how they would ordinarily behave with a new boyfriend in the flesh. Because of the many chats people have, theoretically, a relationship can build over time. This is good because people get the opportunity to get to know someone well before they lose themselves in love.

However, a girl doesn't really know whether the person on the other side of the computer is the one he claims to be. He says he's a 19-year-old guy, but could he be an older man? He claims to be in college, but could he really be pumping gas for a living at his local garage? He claims to be heterosexual, but is he really gay? Despite the great potential that can exist in Internet meeting, there are also many dangers to believing you are falling for someone who is making himself seem greater or younger or older or more available than he actually is. To protect yourself, Internet meeting must be done cautiously, and with great care about sharing personal information, especially at first.

Dear Dr. Gilda:

I am 14 and in love with someone off the Internet. I will be able to meet him this summer and he wants to have sex. What should I do?   *Willie*

Dear Willie:

You must be kidding! I receive a lot of letters from unsuspecting girls like yourself who think some character off the 'net is on the up-and-up. Don't fall for that royal line of B.S. Despite all the tender words he e-mails you, this dude can be "N E 1.com." Behind the computer screen a guy could tell you anything—and most of them pump up their social résumé to appear far better than they actually are. I have heard horrible stories from females who were hurt badly by someone off the 'net whom they trusted—physically, emotionally, and financially.

Maybe the guy that you've met is okay, although I

doubt it since he already told you that he wants to have sex on your first date. Check it out: if you tell him you're *not* interested in doing that, I wonder if he'd be just as anxious to visit with you! But, okay, maybe I'm coming down a little hard on someone we don't know. What would be safe is to spend a lot of time having conversations over the telephone with him. I mean a *lot* of time! Listen to him talk about things that are important to him, stuff that makes him mad, people he loves, folks he dislikes.

You mention your own age, but you don't mention his. Be sure you find that out, as well, before you jump to any more conclusions. For all you know, he could be some 50-year-old pervert coming on as a young Romeo. Be sure you see a photo of him, also. Of course, I've heard of guys sending photos of someone other than themselves. I've heard of horrific lies that guys tell unsuspecting females, and I've known about a few murders from Internet meetings. If you feel that you can trust this character after playing detective, then you can agree to meet in a *public* place. For added security, have a friend with you. Don't let him stay over at your home. If he's interested in you as a person, rather than as an easy sex target, he'll walk through walls to meet you, greet you, and try to make you happy. The ball is in your court. Please be smart.

Dr. Gilda

Questions like Willie's upset me. She is young and trusting, and who is there to protect an innocent girl from characters she may meet on the Internet? This is when I want to run courses exclusively for teenage girls in It Girl training. Remember, It Girls know their value, and they won't put up with anything but the very best!

But some 'net girls are unwilling to heed the warnings, and plow on ahead in record speed:

Dear Dr. Gilda:

I met this guy in cyber about two months ago. The relationship went fast. He asked me to marry him and I said 'yes.' We will meet in June. But now, he is not so attentive anymore and not as charming as he used to be. Perhaps he is too sure of me. I think also that at times he is not being totally honest with me about how he spends his time. I am so confused and I know I can't talk to him about this. What am I to do?   *Cyber Girl*

Dear Cyber:

How lucky that you didn't meet him yet! You rushed things along so fast that in two months you were ready to walk down the aisle for the rest of your life!! This is crazy! Isn't your future worth more than having *any* guy?

I think you're real lucky. This character is beginning to show his true colors. If you already suspect he's not being honest with you while he's courting you and supposedly on his best behavior, go with your gut. You can't marry someone you don't know. But then again, you're getting to know a lot more about him than you did at first.

I'd say cut your losses and run in the opposite direction. Next time go for a guy you can see face-to-face. Or don't you feel good enough about yourself to show your face in public?? Honey, nothing good is without some hassles. Ya gotta put in the time with a guy to see if it's even worth the effort to continue. That kind of time requires in-person dates over a long period. Thank your lucky stars that you saw the light before it was too late!

Dr. Gilda

Flush away the Bad Boy Attraction

I receive so much mail from girls who are wild about "bad boys." They're the guys who steal your heart, can't be trusted, lie, cheat, and diss you every chance they get. Forget about thinking this guy is Prince Charming; he's really the *Lying King*! Although some of these baddies are quite enticing, few of them are very nice.

Dear Dr. Gilda:

Earlier I wrote about being desperate for one of two different guys. Well, the one who's free still ignores me, but today, for some reason, the one who is taken was a total flirt! There is a dance coming up at our school and he said he would dance with me and my two other buddies. I felt so great—until I found out he might dump his girl for my friend. I am so jealous. How can I show him a good time at the dance and win him away without her knowing? Of course, if she went out with him, she would still be a good friend. She doesn't know he likes her yet, and deep inside I don't want her to know. I have a week and two days until this dance. Is there something I can do at school? Help me!   *Lost with Love*

Dear Lost with Love:

First of all, I don't like to hear that you're feeling "desperate" for love. Besides, why would you want either of these two specimens? One doesn't know you're breathing, and the other flirts with anything wearing a skirt. Neither of them sounds like he'd be a caring boyfriend for you. Do you really want to be involved with either of these losers? Why are you not seeking guys who are totally, 100 percent available to you? Do you not think you're worth it? When you go after unavailable dudes, you're really saying that you're willing to take *anyone*. Is that the rep you want? Tell yourself:

Gilda Gram   If it's not easy, I don't need it.

> Then be sure to run, not walk, from anyone who gives you a hard time. Love is beautiful, but you'll never know that if you continue to set yourself up for heartache. Come on, girl, give yourself a break! *Dr. Gilda*

Letting go is a struggle for a lot of girls. To let go of a guy, a girl has to admit to herself that:

Gilda Gram

It's not important to be part of *a* couple. It's more important to be part of *the right* couple.

Experts say it takes twenty-one days to let go of a habit. Affairs of the heart may take a bit longer to dismiss. But like giving up smoking, it's well worth the hassle in the end.

If you're ready to say bye-bye to someone who has not been treating you right, make a promise to yourself. Tell yourself that you are making a legal, binding agreement that will cost you a lot if you go back on your word. Say, "Self, no matter how he begs, or what he says, this relationship is o-v-e-r. I am not going back to him no matter what." To be sure you're not tempted, screen your calls, take alternate routes to school and work so you definitely won't run into him, and follow the 3-Step Take Care Plan: Get Busy, Get Solo, Get Friendly. You've had enough pain being involved with this jerk. Now you can protect yourself from future hurt.

As you begin to move on without him, of course you'll

suffer the emptiness. After all, you weren't crazy. There were some great reasons you were with him. Remember the good times you had together, but don't fool yourself into forgetting the pain. Whatever you do, realize that your blues won't last forever. In fact,

Gilda Gram   Feeling the blues, like feeling hungry, is only a temporary condition.

But unless you enjoy being miserable, it's up to you to make the awful feelings disappear.

Start your healing process by developing the skills you need to size up the next guys you meet. Learn to quickly identify their stay-away traits. Bad boys aren't interested in treating girls well. They make girls feel horrible. They do things that are unacceptable, things that are illegal, things that are immoral. How can you identify a bad boy? For starters, they sometimes look and sound bad. Often you can tell from what they say, how they look, and what they wear that you should keep your distance. Sometimes bad boys will be withdrawn and moody. Other times they will be hostile and angry. These are pretty obvious personality types to avoid. But sometimes, bad boys look like the boy next door. They offer you sweet, compelling lines that would make any girl's heart sink. These Romeos have their badness down to a science, and girls unknowingly flip out. Don't let that happen to you. Guys with those sugar-sweet cover-ups are the bad boys you especially have to be on your guard against.

Dear Dr. Gilda:

I recently made out with my friend's 20-year-old brother. My question is, could he possibly have any feelings for me, even though he's 7 years older than I am? Or is he just using me? Help!!   *Jaime*

Dear Jaime:

I hate to tell you this, but there are laws that make it illegal for this guy to be abusing a minor. In other words, he could be arrested. He's much too old for you and of course he's taking advantage of your innocence, which you already know, or you wouldn't have asked this question. What could a 13-year-old possibly have to talk about with a *man* of 20? (Although, now that I've used the word *man,* I must reconsider that. Is he retarded, immoral, or just plain stupid?)

I know it feels great to know that you can attract an older guy. But there's something wrong with him if he thinks he can have a relationship with someone your age. In a few years, the difference in your ages won't matter so much, but for now, fortunately, the law protects you against your own naïveté. Please, please find a guy more appropriate to your age so you won't get hurt.   *Dr. Gilda*

This guy is the brother of someone Jaime calls a "friend." Presumably her friend knows that Jaime and her brother connected. As a friend's older brother, he could appear like he's a reliable bet. Jaime must be very cautious, because obviously her friend is not doing anything to protect her. What we learn from this example is that no matter how terrific your friends may seem, or how sweet and appropriate a guy may appear, ultimately:

Gilda Gram   It's up to you to take care of yourself.

No one is going to look out for you the way you will look out for yourself. So become your own caretaker, your own protector. This is what It Girls do. They show their strong inner self. By sharpening her awareness skills, a girl will be better able to identify the characteristics of a bad boy. But even if she's missed the signs (everybody makes mistakes), she'll be able to get herself out of a tough situation if she should find herself in one. This is important, because as smart as she may be, bad boys can be found anywhere, especially in places you least expect them.

Bad boys who have absolutely no regard for their steady girlfriends, or even the children they have together, are dangerous. There are plenty of losers who swear they are committed to a girl, yet who don't follow through on their words. Keeping these guys around is NOT—I repeat, NOT—the way to create excitement in your life.

Dear Dr. Gilda:

I really hope that you can help me give a friend of mine a wake-up call. Here's the situation. Carole is 19 and dating this guy who has another girlfriend who he's living with and has a child with. Carole has been seeing him for two years now and ever since day one he has been telling her how bad things are with his live-in girlfriend (He started seeing my friend before he moved in with the other one.) At the beginning everything was wonderful. They went everywhere together and he was very loving. But since moving in with this other girl, they've had a baby together (so things can't be that bad!). Recently, he started neglecting Carole. To compete with the other girl, Carole got her own apartment in the hope that he would start spending more time with her. Well, it didn't work. Now she wants to have his baby, also, although she insists that it's not to compete with the other girl. She says that she wants a baby even if he doesn't, as long as he will spend time with his child as it grows up. When I told her to look for someone who cares for her as much as she cares for him, she responded that things were good enough for her as they were.

Dr. Gilda, I have tried to talk to her and give her advice. But since the advice I give her is not what she wants to hear, she has completely shut me out. What can I do to make her see that she should have higher standards where guys are concerned? This is not her first bad-boy relationship. She had spent five years with a married man.

She mopes around in hopes that this guy will show up. Please help. I don't want to see her get hurt.   *Gisele*

Dear Gisele:

Wow! Carole is a mess, and the best thing she's got going for her is YOU. As much as you try to reason with her, it does no good. I can understand how frustrated you must feel. If she thinks a baby will keep this guy coming around, she's really setting herself up for a letdown. As it is, she already refuses to believe that this guy doesn't give a rat's tail about her. Yet you say that she mopes around hoping he'll change. Good luck, Carole!

Girls who continually seek out such bad boys don't believe they are good enough to attract a cool guy who will care about them. This is apparently Carole's pattern, and nothing you can do will change her.

You have tried to offer your advice. But you can't help someone who doesn't want to be helped. I suggest you find another friend with whom you have more things in common. You're not your friend's teacher or preacher. Get on with your own life, and let Carole learn the hard way that friends like you are golden, and bad boys never change—unless *they* see the need.   *Dr. Gilda*

Lots of girls long to find friendships that are as loving as this one. Gisele really cares about her buddy, but Carole doesn't care about *herself*. For all of us, there's a point at which we have to let go and let our friends fend for themselves. As hard as it sounds, if their ship sinks, it's their doing, and you, as their friend, must choose to move on.

I get thousands of letter from girls who *refuse* to heed the bad-boy warnings. It's very frustrating to get one letter after another, all with the message that some guy either abuses a girl, tells her lies, has sex with her and discards her, is mean to her, or ignores her entirely—*yet she still loves him!! Duhhhhhh!!*

Dear Dr. Gilda:

My boyfriend just broke up with me a week ago. We had been going out for six months. He says I didn't treat him special enough. But really he's the one with the problem. I did more for him than he ever did for me. Then, he mentally abused me. But I still love him and want him back. What should I do?   *Jane*

Dear Jane:

This guy mentally abused you, gave you little compassion, and complained that you didn't do enough for him? Sorry, but he doesn't need a girlfriend; he needs a mommy with a nipple. Nobody will ever be able to make him happy.

Many girls get into your situation misbelieving that

if only they could make their miserable boyfriend happy, then they'd be happy, too. Actually, they learn after some time that the more they try to change themselves to make their guy happy, the less they respect themselves . . . and, interestingly, the less their guy respects them. Really, you should thank your lucky stars because this dude did you a favor by leaving you. Now if you could only recognize what love really is, because that's what will provide the only reasons for you to give away your heart.

Gilda Gram   People who love you don't hurt you.

Jane, we don't love a guy who mentally abuses us, gives us little to go on, then complains we're not giving enough. No, Jane. If we do, your boyfriend's right, it's we who have the problem. As much as you claim the problem lies with your ex, you can claim the booby prize for stupidity for wanting him back ANYWAY! Get a life!!   *Dr. Gilda*

Dear Dr. Gilda:

I have known and liked this guy for seven months. He wanted to keep it friends because he's a bad boy and he thought I was too "good." Well, we have this thing going where we have "fun" in private, but we don't tell anyone because he doesn't want to be tied down right now. I know I am not the only girl he's interested in or seeing right now, but I am the one who he knows the best. I really like him and I can't get him off my mind. I know he likes me as a friend and maybe more. What should I do to make a move he can't refuse? I can be exactly what he wants.   *Stephanie*

Dear Stephanie:

This guy is giving you no encouragement, yet you're willing to jump through hoops for him. Exactly what kind of move "he can't refuse" did you have in mind? And let's say you decide to make that move. Do you really think that that will keep him? What scares me is the statement that you're willing to become anything he wants. What are you, a blob of Silly Putty? Have you lost your mind? But then again, did you ever have one? If you're so willing to change your whole self for a guy, I guess your self wasn't so strong and sturdy to begin with.

Right now this guy likes you as a friend just as you are. But you've also got to recognize that he's using you for sex while he's also getting it elsewhere. If you think that all being loved takes is to change yourself to the specifications a guy wants, you are setting yourself up for major letdown.

Instead of going after someone who's emotionally unavailable to you, find a guy who is ready, willing, and able to let you into his life. With the right guy, you won't have to redecorate yourself. Then, and only then, will you know you've grown up.   *Dr. Gilda*

Dear Dr. Gilda:

I really like this guy I work with, but he is always mean to me. Usually he doesn't talk to me at all. Help me, please. I really like him a lot.   *Rosemary*

Dear Rosemary:

Please fill me in here. Exactly what do you like about someone who is mean to you and usually ignores you? How can you say that you even *know* him, much less *like* him? Would you like a girlfriend who treated you this way? You really do need help. But I'm not the one to give it to a girl who's in la-la land. Grow up!   *Dr. Gilda*

When girls want guys who are not emotionally available to them, it suggests that the girls are not secure in themselves to believe that they deserve more. Sometimes these girls will put up with horrendous treatment and still return for more of the same; other times they will attempt to make themselves irreplaceable by becoming the guy's nursemaid. In their minds, if they "save" him from himself, he'll undoubtedly be ever grateful and never leave. *Fat chance!*

Dear Dr. Gilda:

I see your talk shows all the time and you are great. Here is my question. I am dating this guy I like very much. He is 19 and I'm 18. He's sweet and treats me with respect. The only thing is that he doesn't go to school and he smokes weed. I think that by being around him I can change him because when he's with me he doesn't do it. I feel I'm a good influence on him. Can there be any hope?

My boyfriend says he wants to do something with his life. But I ask, when is he going to start? He's already 19 and doesn't have a high school diploma. Could he be saying this as a front? I'm trying to talk him into getting his GED. How can I get it through his head that he needs an education? I really don't know why I fall for these kind of guys. I just think I find them attractive and I want to help them.

Ginger

Dear Ginger:

The only question you should be asking is the last: why you fall for these kind of guys. Trying to be Florence Nightingale to your boyfriend is taking needed focus away from what you must do with your own life. You are right; when is this guy going to grow up? You're also right in knowing that talk is cheap. Behavior is the only thing that counts—and your Prince Charming is not doing anything to indicate that his behavior is changing.

The answer to your most important question is that you feel better about yourself when you make your guy into a project that puts you at center stage. Give that up. Emphasize your *own* goals. When you do, you will attract a different breed of guy, someone who adores you for having been so directed and accomplishing so much. The two of you will be on the same level, without either of you having to feel elevated while the other is still crawling. The time to start is immediately, because you have already wasted too much time on this loser.

Dr. Gilda

The reason I showed you these letters is that I want you, the reader, to get as fed up with these girls' acceptance of poor treatment as I am. What, exactly, do these girls like—or love—about these guys? What feedback are they getting that these guys are even remotely interested in being committed to them? What makes them think, as Stephanie said, that if she becomes "exactly what he wants" he'll think any differently of her? Although she's interested in making "a move he can't refuse," she's already putting her body on the line for him. And that hasn't made him more interested in her. What else would Stephanie like to do to prove she cares? Steal? Rob? Murder?? These guys are keeping these girls in relationship hell. *But it's the girls who agree to stay there.* So,

Gilda Gram

The question is not what's wrong with your bad boy. It's *what's wrong with you???*

It's always easy to point the finger of blame at the boys for being bad. But girls have to accept the responsibility for allowing these guys to continue their antics with them. In reality:

Gilda Gram   Bad boys don't just *take* from girls. They are *given.*

So before you develop ulcers over a guy who's trouble, sit down, look yourself in the mirror, and say, "I accept my role in this relationship." As the saying goes, "It takes two to tango." So if you're grief-stricken enough over some dude, all you've got to do is remove one person from the dance, and see how tough it is for your guy to boogie without you.

But also let's understand what girls find so attractive about bad boys. Bad boys attract nice girls because their badness is exciting. They provide a drama that makes every female drama queen ecstatic. The walk on the wild side is thrilling to girls whose lives are more ordinary. The girls mistake the heart-pumping excitement they feel for love.

This is where being alone and having time to think about what is really happening to you is crucial. This is the time to recognize:

Gilda Gram   If a guy's doing something *to* you rather than *for* you, it's time to pack him in.

Sure, the guys these girls describe are snakes. But who is it that allows them such privileges with their minds and bodies? *Once again, it's the girls themselves!*

Girls who like bad boys have serious dating disorders. More specifically, they don't think highly enough about themselves to believe they could snag a cool guy. They don't believe that their own lives can be exciting on their own, and they mistakenly think that they need a guy to pump up the volume. Also, these girls probably haven't seen positive relationship role models that are respectful and caring. Put all these factors together and you have innocent girls who are easily misled.

If you notice, these girls know something is not right, and they're miserable enough to contact me and ask for help. But they don't understand that they must also help themselves. They've got to find their own adventure in life. They've got to explore their own passions. They've got to say no to being ignored or mistreated. They've got to surround themselves with positive relationships that work. In fact, before they fall in with any guy, they must screen them to see if these guys are even *worthy* of the girls' efforts and emotions. But to do that, the girls must have high self-confidence, a strong inner self, and boundaries that they stick to.

Too many girls use the excuse, "I know I have low self-esteem." If that's the case, THEN RAISE IT! They confess, "I don't think I'm worth anything without a guy." If that's the case, THEN CHANGE THAT. Girls must be strong enough to choose to do the things that *they* want to do, no matter what pressure they get from their guys to do otherwise. They must tell themselves—and believe—that they have *high* self-esteem. They must think that they are fine, alone, without a guy. This way, when a cool guy appears, they are pleasantly surprised, and cool themselves. Cool girls can handle cool guys without a care in the world.

Are you one of those girls who is attracted to a bad boy? Take this Bad–Boy Screener and discover the truth!

BAD-BOY SCREENER

Answer Yes or No to each of the following questions:

———— 1. Are you mostly attracted to guys who ignore you?

———— 2. Do you find yourself going along with the plans of guys you don't even respect?

———— 3. Do the guys you like often hit on your girlfriends?

———— 4. Do you constantly tell yourself that although he's bad, you know he'll change?

———— 5. Do the guys you like call you bad names, criticize your body, and diss you?

———— 6. Do the guys you like rarely call you?

———— 7. Do the guys you like lie to you or sneak around behind your back?

———— 8. Do the guys you like get into trouble at school or with the law?

———— 9. Do the guys you like have secret lives that few people know about?

_____ **10.** Do the guys you like have bad relations with their parents?

_____ **11.** Do the guys you like constantly compare you to their ex?

_____ **12.** Do the guys you like take everything you say personally and defensively?

_____ **13.** Do the guys you like exhibit a bad case of roving eye?

Score Card

Surprise! If you had even one yes, you're a bad-boy magnet. If you want a happy relationship, it's time you change your tastes. Begin by telling yourself:

Gilda Gram   I deserve a cool guy.

Then take action.

Girls are notorious for wanting to change their boyfriends, even the ones who are not the traditional bad boys. They think, my guy would be so cool—if only he'd change his taste in music to hard rock; if only he'd change his baggy jeans to cargo pants; if only he'd change his love for the History Channel to MTV. It's as though their guys are not good enough as they are when they meet them, so the girls think they'll do a makeover on them and make them better. In truth, nobody changes just because someone else wants him to. If you think a guy will go for an overhaul of any kind, give that up! If anything, most guys will resent a girl trying to mess with something she shouldn't. In all fairness, girls could learn a thing or two from guys in this regard.

Remember the guy-pleasing girls we discussed earlier? As soon as a guy enters the picture, she does a makeover on herself. A girl with a strong inner self wouldn't put up with that any more than a guy would put up with a girl trying to change him. So, whether your guy is a bad boy or not, lay off him. He's like that dress on the rack, a little holey, a little soiled, but the price is marked "as is." Take it or leave it. Similarly, take or leave your guy as you find him. Because *unless he sees a need to change*, the way he is is the way he's going to stay!

Guys can and do change *if they themselves want to*. To be totally fair, before you give your bad boy his walking papers, take these quik-steps to see if your dude could become a *recovering* bad boy, a bad boy of the past, who sees the errors of his ways and is ready and willing to become respectful and cool.

Quick-Steps to Take Before You Walk Out

1. Confront your guy in a calm mood. Be sure to follow the 3-step "When you . . . , I feel . . . , Stop" technique.

2. Know in advance what your boundaries are: What will you accept and what won't you tolerate? For example, know that if he hits you, you're out for sure—and there's no turning back. Know also that you won't allow yourself to be

dragged into your nasty guy's tirades. Finally, be unwilling to play the blame game where you return his anger with your anger. That's nonproductive and an energy waste. Besides, it will get you nowhere for the next time he pulls his antics.

3. Let him know that if he doesn't clean up his act, you're out of there. Many bully boys back down when they see their girlfriends will no longer take on the role of victim who lets them get away with their nonsense. Tell him exactly what you need and expect from him so he can't come back to you later and say he didn't know. But be sure that once you give him the ultimatum of walking, you *keep your word.* So before you say anything, you must be sure that this is your now-or-never strategy. Otherwise, your word won't count for anything, and your guy will continue his badness toward you for as long as you're together.

Once you've tried everything, you may see that your bad boy chooses to remain as he is. Then you have two choices: accept him as he is or leave. Whatever you decide to do is your choice. If you accept your boyfriend the way he is, you give up the right to try to change him and the luxury of spending endless hours with your friends complaining about him. For one thing, your friends will get tired of hearing the same sickening spiel ad nauseam without your taking action. Do you want to lose your good buds?

Also recognize that if you decide to stay, you have chosen the kind of relationship for which you are willing to settle. Does that sound awful? Deal with reality. Remember from our earlier chapters, any girl who willingly accepts "Less-Than" Treatment from a guy is accepting it, and thereby teaching him that it's okay to continue treating her the way he has all along. Since you're not chained to this dude, you must admit that if you're still with him after such bad treatment, you have wholeheartedly agreed to go along with the program. Now that you've been reminded, is it still 100 percent all right with you to continue the relationship? Or, do you think you'd prefer to leave?

If you decide to leave, remember that you'll need some time to be without anyone. You'll need time alone to figure out, "What did I see in him, anyway?" Why did I originally think he was dateworthy?" And now, "What even makes him buzzworthy?" After you have completely recovered from the whole ordeal, you'll be ready to try again. That's when you need to retrain your tastes about the benefits of having a cool guy.

How to Recognize the Cool Guys

Take some time alone to consider how to attract relatively stress-free relationships with guys who treat you well. What makes a guy "cool?" What do cool guys look like? How do they act? How do they treat a girl? Drew Barrymore says, "A great boyfriend doesn't pee on your parade. . . . He'll get out of the car and pick you a few flowers." Brandy says, "It's the little things that count—like a phone call when you least expect it." Once you can recognize what good-guy behavior looks like in other relationships, you'll be on your way to attracting a cool guy yourself. To help you find that cool guy, follow the Cool Guy Selector.

Cool Guy Selector

How do you know if he's a cool guy? The traits cool guys demonstrate are:

1. Attentiveness
2. Affection
3. Devotion
4. Compassion
5. Dependability
6. Generosity
7. Loyalty
8. Trust
9. Honesty
10. Stability
11. Fidelity

In addition to these basics, cool guys will want to care for you when you're sick; compliment you when you look good or do something well; enjoy your friends and family; be happy when something makes you happy; remember special occasions; enjoy spending quiet nights together, but give you your space to be alone; use the pronouns *we, us,* and *ours,* and generally treat you with respect. Sometimes cool guys are so cool that girls tend to take them for granted. That's a big mistake, because if you don't crush on a cool guy, a wiser girl will. No girl would possibly have time to consider seeking these traits in a guy if she's constantly out and about, especially with losers. This is why quiet time alone is so important.

Clean the Clutter

The great thing about being with a cool guy is that he appreciates all the different aspects of your life. He's a part of your heart, but he's not the sole reason you get up in the morning. Remember that one of the qualities a cool guy finds attractive in a girl is her independence and ability to be self-sufficient. Girls who can fend for themselves are usually well organized, making it easier to excel at what they do. Are you someone whose life is well organized? Can you find what you need when you need it? Look at your closets. Check out your desk. Evaluate your room. Although your neatness may seem like a superficial habit, it actually says a lot about your ability to open your life to greater challenges, which, in turn, make you more interesting to the cool guys. For example, do you tend to save everything you own? That suggests that you might hold on to boyfriends and girlfriends long after you've realized you've outgrown them. Look at those piles of papers on your desk, the cases of makeup scattered around your room, your overstuffed and piled-high closet. Messiness suggests you want to hang on to things that clutter your life.

So what's the big deal? The way you collect things may show that you also collect people in the same way. Here's a news flash: when you surround yourself with clutter, you don't have available space for new things. Now apply this example to the people you know. If you hang on to people who are not your greatest supporters, you don't have room for those who could be.

The cure? Get rid of the clutter that surrounds your immediate space so you can open your life to better *people* to love you. Doesn't it feel great after you've cleaned your room, or your closets, or your makeup case? You suddenly can "see" again. You can find things you had misplaced. Of course, you'll have the luxury of making your space messy again, but this time with new and different things, things that represent the *new* you.

After you've done a reorganization, you become clear about what you want and where you're going. Your goals are clearer, your dreams are more vivid, and you'll have the room to attract people who are real. You're able to schedule time for many things you thought you didn't have time for before. And you find time for more varied activities, especially the ones you had put on hold. You find yourself going to the gym more often, and taking care of your body. That makes you feel good. You see friends you haven't seen, attend only the events that make you happy, and become more selective about what you do. In other words, by rearranging your space, you give yourself greater exposure to the fabulous people out there who you never knew. That's the first step to loving yourself.

How to Love the Person You Are

Who are you? I mean, who is the *real* you? Don't describe your outside packaging. Your blond hair, green eyes, long legs, or any other external attributes don't count. Neither does your pimply skin, frizzy hair, or ten extra pounds. We're not talking about the external traits that often make girls feel inadequate for not competing with airbrushed or computer-generated images on the cover of your fave magazine. Besides, these attributes are not *who you are*. Who you are consists of your inner-self traits, like your devotion to animals, your humorous view of the world, your kindness toward the elderly. Devotion, humor, and kindness are just a few of the inner-self qualities that really describe you.

Close your eyes. Describe who you are: _____
_____
_____
_____

This is a very difficult exercise to complete because we're so used to thinking in terms of external attributes. After some coaxing, here are some responses from girls with strong inner selves:

"I have a strong will. I won't allow myself to be misled."

"I know my power, and I don't let anyone try to take it away from me."

"I am nurturing, but before I give in to other people, I first nurture myself."

Here are some other responses from girls who need to develop inner-self muscle:

"I am shy and quiet, so most people tend to take advantage of me."

"I'm a pushover for people when they pressure me."

"When I'm with my friends, I keep my opinions to myself, even when I know I'm right."

If your responses do not express the *real* you, take another look. Understand that you are beautiful just as you are—faults and all. And your beauty is more than skin deep. Know that, appreciate that, honor that.

Once you are feeling independent and self-sufficient, you'll know that you don't *need* a boyfriend. You will believe in yourself for all your wonderful inner qualities. That feeling of being secure will show itself on the outside. You won't have to have a soulmate. In fact, you'll be happy for a while with a guy who's simply a teammate. What follows after that is anyone's guess.

NEED #4

Make Him a Teammate Before a Soulmate

On the popular TV series *Dawson's Creek*, Joey and Dawson had been great friends for an entire season. It wasn't until the first year's season finale that they finally kissed. Viewers watched their friendship slowly turn to love. Now they've seen the pair come together, break up, make up, and generally go through the usual teenage relationship ups and downs. Most teens can certainly identify with the duo:

Dear Dr. Gilda:

I am really in need of your help! There is this guy in my class, and we have been friends forever, like Dawson and Joey. Last month he asked me out. After I said no, he was heartbroken. Now we don't talk. That was a month ago. I've decided that I really like him after all, and I want to go out with him, but I don't know if he still likes me. I am too shy to ask him out. What if he says no? I can't take the risk. Please help me!!   *Kate*

 Gilda Gram   Friendship with a guy is a first and necessary step to more.

Dear Kate:

If you and your guy were really great friends, you would feel more comfortable about bridging the gap between your palship and your potential love. Obviously, he knows that something's up between you because he asked you out. He would never have taken that bold step if he thought he'd be rejected. But you surprised possibly both of you by saying no. As any insecure teenage guy would do, he backed off. What did you expect him to do?

Now you say you've changed your mind. Since you're not sure whether he still likes you, and he apparently refused to endure another humiliation, you've got to swallow your pride and level with him. (Don't worry, he won't bite your head off.) Tell him the truth, that his invitation caught you by surprise, and now you'd like to reconsider. If he's into playing games now, he may try to give you back some of your own medicine. But if he's really a good friend, he'll level with you back. It's certainly worth a shot because the way things are now, he'll never know that you'd like to reconsider. Good luck.   *Dr. Gilda*

I receive many letters from girls who want to advance their relationship a notch or two with their guy friends. In fact, friends who want to become lovers is probably one of my largest categories of correspondence. The letters come from teenagers of all ages all over the world. Each one expresses the fear of ruining a terrific friendship if the romance tanks:

Dear Dr. Gilda:

How do I tell a guy I love him when he's my best friend?

May

Dear Dr. Gilda:

All the guys I have ever liked are my really good friends and wouldn't date me. How do I make them realize I can be more than a friend?

Ellie

Dear Dr. Gilda:

Hello! I'm in love with my best friend. We just recently became great friends, but I trust him with my life and I tell him everything. Sometimes it seems as though we're a couple. But I don't know if he feels the same way. I'm afraid that if I say anything, our friendship would become weird. I don't want to lose his friendship, but I really do have deep feelings for him. What do I do? Should I tell him or just wait until if—and when—he makes a move himself?   *Star*

Dear Dr. Gilda:

I have fallen in love with my best guy friend. He doesn't know how I feel about him. Should I tell him or keep it to myself? This situation happened to me once before and it ended up turning out horrible. I was really into one of my other guy friends, he ended up finding out, and he didn't like me as a girlfriend. Now we don't even talk much anymore. I guess I'm afraid of this happening to me again! What should I do? I don't want to ruin our friendship. I'm ready to burst!! Is there any way I can change the way I feel? Please help me!

Dazed and Confused in LA

Sometimes it's the other way around, with a girl writing to me about some guy she's really not attracted to as a boyfriend, but he's a fab friend:

Dear Dr. Gilda:

I have this one friend who I really like. Well, the other day, he asked me out on a date. I just wanna stay friends. What do I do?   *Cathy*

But just in case you think this is only a girl's problem, think again. Guys also have questions about taking a relationship to the next step:

Dear Dr. Gilda:

I have been friends with this girl for three years now and I am starting to have strong feelings for her. My question is, how do I go about asking her out? If she doesn't feel the same, I don't want to scare her off and lose a good friend.

Don

So what's the deal? If a girl spills the beans and the guy's even remotely interested, all's well and good. They begin dating, and they see what happens. But if she wears her heart on her sleeve and the guy rejects her, her heart *becomes* her sleeve, as she finds herself using it to wipe her eyes and nose. If a girl takes the plunge and loses, not only has she lost a possible love, she's also lost a dear friend. As we all know, good friends—especially guy friends—are hard to come by. So before a girl risks it all, she must be more sure about the outcome. Of course, nobody can predict someone else's behavior. But a girl needs to look for clues before she pushes for more. So how can a girl get herself promoted from friend to girlfriend?

Clues That Suggest a Possible Future

1. He keeps his word about calling when he promises to.
2. He gives you details about his life and doesn't mention other girls.
3. He mentions something he'd like to do with you next week.
4. He cracks up at your jokes.
5. His looks into your eyes become longer and more intense.
6. His hand on your hand or your shoulder lingers longer than usual.
7. He programmed your number at the top of the list of his cell phone's speed dial.
8. Friends say he talks about you when you're not around.
9. He waits for you after school.
10. He gave you an intimate gift for your birthday.
11. He notices your new haircut.
12. He doesn't introduce you as his "friend," but uses your name instead.
13. He talks to you on the phone for hours.
14. He'd rather hang with you than anyone else.

Of course, these signs mean that you and your guy are great friends. Without reading into any of the cues, he could simply be acting *very* friendly. And you may be harboring great expectations that will blow up in your face. Or, as much as he's trying to hide it, he may actually be thinking "she's lots of fun" and moving toward "she's the one." How do you snag him into "Whoa . . . I'm in love"?

Don't suggest outright that the two of you date. Remember, he's the hunter and hunters like to do the hunting without a girl's help. Just keep in mind that people communicate by three means:

1. Body language
2. Voice
3. Words

Saying the wrong thing can make a girl feel uncomfortable at best, and humiliated at worst. So stay away from the use of sappy words unless you decide to use that approach after all else has failed. But first, try using your body language and vocal tones. The most important thing to remember is to continue to be yourself. That means don't put this guy on a pedestal thinking he'll emerge from "friend" to "boyfriend." Use your humor to continue to enjoy each other. Remember, since this guy is your friend, he already appreciates your personality. You just want him to love it in a different way. If it's going to happen, it will take some time. As the song goes, "You can't hurry love." So what's the rush?

First, body language. Get him alone and offer up some melt-him moves he won't forget. Let your shoulder touch his while you're discussing homework. Look deep into his eyes. Smile. *The man will know something's changed . . . and something's up.* Support your body moves with soft, sweet sounds of smiling words that have nothing to do with the two of you. Yes, always wear a smiling attitude. It's a superpowered guy-magnet. If your body language and voice are working, you'll see:

Immediate Signs of Encouragement

1. You're out as "friends," but he insists on paying his share and yours.

2. His face turns red and he stutters when he's near you.

3. His body language moves in sync with yours. For example, if your legs are crossed, so are his. If one of your hands is in your pocket, so is his. In other words, he outright copies you, girl. That's the highest form of flattery.

These immediate encouragement signals tell you he's probably beginning to come around. Now don't you blow it by acting too aggressive, taking the reins away from him, and scaring him off. Your objective is to charm him, not alarm him. So be patient—and have some staying power. Keep in mind that he's as uncomfortable about being rejected as you are. Let the relationship unfold naturally. Keep sending him body language and vocal signs of interest. He'll know what you're doing, and if he's interested, he will come around.

Okay, you've waited long enough, and you've tried just about everything. The guy just doesn't get it. Now it's time to resort to using words. Again, you don't want to feel foolish, so instead of suggesting the two of you become an item, float a test balloon: "David [always use his name for closeness and to let him know you're serious], could you imagine what would happen if we were ever a couple?" Let his dense head sift through the thought. If he dismisses the idea quickly, he's probably not interested. If he lightly laughs it off, there may be some hope. If he strongly says, "We'd never make it together. You're too demanding, and so am I," you know he might have had a fleeting thought about it, but has determined that it just can't work. Once a guy is dead set against a relationship, even if you stripped naked and professed your undying love for him, his no means no and you don't want to push it. (On second thought, if you did strip naked for him, he would probably agree to have sex with you—but walk out anyway. Who needs that?) But that's not to say he won't change his mind somewhat down the road. It's just that for now, this dude's off limits, and it's best to keep the relationship strictly on a friendship basis.

Let's suggest another possibility: you're already a team, but it's been a while since you first started dating. Since you've been together, he's never said anything to indicate this is a permanent thing. You know he dates other girls from time to time, but you want a committed relationship already. What is a girl to do?

To Commit or Split?

He's thinking "fling," while for you it's the "real thing." Obviously, the two of you are experiencing two different relationships while you're both in the same one! So how do you get him to get on track? How can you move him along to make you his one and only?

You probably won't like my answer to this dilemma. It's one that most girls need some training in. The word is *patience.* Of course, if you've already determined that your stud muffin is an out-and-out bad boy who wants to have a bevy of girls around him, there's nothing you can do to change him from a player to a one-woman man. I've showed you the differences between cool guys to choose and bad guys to lose. So bone up on your selection skills to avoid ending up in that jam.

But what if you and your guy are beginning to get close? You see it, you feel it, you know it, although he'd never broach the subject. This is when:

Gilda Gram   Patience is golden.

Dear Dr. Gilda:

Brian is so cool. We go to different schools, but I think he likes me. How long should I wait until I ask him out?   *Mimi, 14*

Dear Mimi:

If you're an It Girl, you're immersed in the activities you love. You won't just wait around for your dude to make a move. You must see Brian somewhere to know that he likes you. But you're so busy, you forget to even think of him from time to time. The best thing to do is to find out about the activities he enjoys. Do you share any of these in common? With those as a starting place, talk about your mutual loves. Remember, guys adore girls who are interested. Immerse yourself in your mutual interests, and if he's interested in you, he's sure to come around.

Dr. Gilda

At the start of a relationship, a girl should research a guy's behaviors. She should be building a friendship as she determines whether she even wants him as a permanent fixture in her life. It's like taking notes on a particular subject. Jot down the pros and cons of his behaviors, the things you like, the things he says. It's just *research*, nothing more, nothing less.

But let's say you're together for a few months. It looks like things are heating up, and so far you like what you see. Even then, although you're giving your guy the cues that you're interested in developing this friendship into something more, again, remember that he's the hunter and you should let the hunter hunt. (I can't say this enough times.) If he takes longer to make a move on you, let him be. Guys operate on guy-time, and nothing you do will get him to pick up the pace. If anything, it could backfire where he feels utterly controlled and manipulated, and can't get away from you soon enough. So before you open your mouth and confront his slowness, give it a reasonable amount of time. What's "reasonable" to you, naturally, may not be "reasonable" to your turtle-like guy. But he's not *all that*. Concentrate on the other things you've got going for you. Rekindle those passions for the things that turn you on—whether he comes around or not.

When girls aren't patient, they get hurt:

Dear Dr. Gilda:

I'm 19, and I really want a long relationship with someone. I've been in love before but things didn't work out. That was two years ago. I can't seem to find someone with whom I can have a good, solid relationship. Every guy today seems not to want commitment.

Sara

Dear Sara:

Isn't it amazing that you keep finding commitment-phobic guys who are cold about getting close? I find that girls who really want to settle down find guys with the same goals. Since we attract people like ourselves, ask yourself whether you're absolutely certain you want a committed guy.

Another possibility is that you seem to want love so badly that you are coming on too strong with the guys you date. Look carefully at your own behavior. Make a list of the qualities in guys you continue to attract. I have a sneaking suspicion that you are projecting cues that are repelling, rather than attracting, the kinds of guys you say you want. Please let me know what you come up with.

Dr. Gilda

Sure enough, Sara came back to me with a list of telltale qualities in three of the guys she had dated for long periods of time. These qualities were obvious to an outsider, but Sara admitted that because she was so intent on hooking up permanently in a committed relationship, she missed them. See if you would pick up on them as don't-go-there cues:

1. A guy who had just broken off a two-year relationship
2. A guy who was moving to another country
3. A guy who was very religious and would only marry into his own faith, of which Sara was not a part

From the list, Sara could readily see that although the guys were generous and kind, they were definitely not commitment-ready. She vowed that on her next dates she'd ask a lot more questions before she'd push to get close. Good for Sara!

Pushing for too much too soon has landed many girls in disaster. I receive letters from a lot of girls after the damage is done. By then, unfortunately, it may be too late:

Dear Dr. Gilda:

There's a guy I've liked for a year and a half. For a couple of months, we've been messing around, sometimes seriously. The problem is, he really doesn't want to commit. I cry a lot when I think that we might part. I enjoy being with him, but I don't want to ask for a commitment because I don't want to scare him off. I've never loved anyone as much as I love him. Everything about him is perfect. We're perfect for each other. Please help.

Susan, 16

Dear Susan:

You're miserable, yet you call this relationship "perfect"? You're living on planet Uranus! You're already "messing around" with him, and from the tone of your letter, I assume he's seeing other girls as well. Messing around, in most cases, means you're having some intimacy. Since you've already been giving your guy the milk, why should he buy the cow? In other words, WIIFM?—or from the guy's point of view, "What's In It For Me?" to want to make a commitment to Susan if I'm already getting everything I want from her? Guys will "mess around" with a mule if it's available, so the fact that *you* love *him* probably means very little to the future of your relationship from his standpoint.

After a year and a half, you've finally got to see that your guy wants to do nothing further with your association. You might try to refrain from being so intimate to determine if that's the only thing holding him to you. But it's about time you found out what's going on in his head. Sure, you might be hurt if he decides to leave, but having spent this much time together already, you don't want it to go on any longer if he's not going to come around. You're only 16. If you don't do something to move this relationship along now, it could continue as is for years.

> So bite the bullet. If your honesty scares your guy away, you know he's an insensitive user, and it's best you find that out now. But if he truly cares for you and doesn't want to lose you, he'll start to think about making a move that's more committed. *Dr. Gilda*

In committed relationships, when two people are giving as much as they are taking, there is less of a possibility that they will be disappointed and hurt. Remember the lesson from *The Little Prince*? Remember how the Little Prince *invested* in the flower, and therefore felt closer to her? When two people have invested time and emotions in the other, neither wants to lose the investment they've built over time. Girls need to wait an appropriate amount of time for their guys to feel "invested" in them. But waiting would not seem an eternity if they eliminated the guy as their central focus and got a life of their own. Unfortunately, Sara wants a relationship so badly she seems desperate. Susan has agreed to "mess around" before her guy is invested in her, so what's his payoff? Girls have to be smart before they put out. Sure, it's a strategy, and some folks call strategies part of playing games. But the point is that the girl should enjoy her life and develop her skills separate and apart from having a boyfriend. Then she won't feel like she's playing games by *saying* she's not available, because she truly won't be.

The impatient and aggressive girl of the new millennium refuses to wait for the hunter to do his thing. She rejects the idea of waiting for the flowers to bloom on their own. So instead, she tugs at the roots, thinking that she will make the plants flower more quickly. Naturally, this can't work. Similarly, when we try to hurry love, we only end up with heartache.

Dear Dr. Gilda:

A group of guys in my school started a rock band. They did a concert last week, and one of the guys, Jason, was singing directly to me. He reminds me so much of Ricky Martin. I really like him, so I sent him a love note with my name and address on it. He still hasn't called. Then I sent him a pair of my panties with my signature. I haven't heard from him yet. What should I do now?

Denise, 17

Dear Denise:

I won't begin by telling you to wait around mindlessly for something to happen with Jason. But you've been very aggressive about how you feel toward him and he never responded. If he hasn't responded yet, what makes you think that he will? When someone is onstage, part of the performance is to flirt with his audience. You bought the act hook, line, and sinker. But you must realize that it was only an act. The proof was when Jason didn't pick up on your cues. If he's really as cute as Ricky Martin, I bet you weren't the only girl who slipped him her telephone number (although I'm not sure about the bit with your panties).

> There's a difference between letting a guy know you're available and being a pest. You don't want Jason to laugh you off as a love-starved chick. So lick your wounds, accept the gig for what it really was, and find someone who is emotionally available, rather than some cute guy singing on a stage, who's out of reach. Who knows? When you least expect it, a real guy who's on the same level as you rather than on a stage could win your heart!
>
> *Dr. Gilda*

Guys need more time to recognize their emotions than girls. Also, girls are more sophisticated than guys when it comes to affairs of the heart. So there's simply no point in rushing something that can't be rushed. Just cool your jets.

Tips for Cooling Your Jets

1. Give him time to discover how valuable you are to him. He must come to this conclusion himself, otherwise he'll feel pressured and run.

2. Stop trying to rush him down the aisle before he's out of diapers. He'll only run faster.

3. Don't become overly emotional. A girl's deep emotions often frighten guys who've been trained to avoid their own vulnerability.

4. Don't try to trick a guy to commit by getting him jealous, getting pregnant, moving in with him, or doing only what he wants to the exclusion of your own needs. When he

realizes these are tricks to try to "get him," he'll move out of your life anyway. Once again, honesty is the only way to go. If he doesn't want you as much as you want him, that's a sign that there's someone better out there for you, and it's time to find him.

4. There are very few guys who won't commit. Be patient and let nature take its course.

There are three little words that suggest the secret for attracting cool guys and making your love work. They are these:

Gilda Gram   Take your time!

When you take your time and stop trying to rush love, you'll be making your guy your teammate instead of trying to push him to become your soulmate. Taking your time will be easy if you are already an It Girl with your own interests. Remember, It Girls don't make guys their central focus because they're into their own thing first.

Teammates are on the same team, with the same goals, the same dreams, the same values. Your guy will feel comfortable knowing that, with you, he doesn't have the love pressure he gets from other girls. He'll see you as a friend he can trust, someone with whom he can be real. He'll show you his feelings, the same feelings he would ordinarily hide from a girl he likes. You'll see him in ways he'll only reveal to his good friends. As you enjoy him for who he really is, he won't act like some insecure teenage guy who's trying to impress a girl. *You'll really know him.*

These kinds of friendships are crucial before real love can set in. That's why I receive so many letters from girls who have been friends with a guy for a long time and now want to take it to the next step. Deep emotional feelings grow from solid friendship. And the best part is, as you get to know him as a teammate, you're in a great position to decide whether you want to pursue something more.

Conclusion

How to Attract the Good Guys

a s you now know, good guys are cool guys, and attracting them is actually very simple. But it's also exactly opposite from what you would expect. It involves focusing on yourself, rather than on a guy. You know this philosophy works, because it's always the guys you have no interest in who are interested in you. Right?

Dear Dr. Gilda:

For the past four years I have liked the same guy. But every time I got close to him, he'd push me away.

Now I'm going into high school, and I've met a guy in the marching band who I like a lot. Since the guy I've liked all these years found out about my new crush, he's been acting very jealous, yet affectionate around me when we hang out. Why is he now finally giving me what I've always wanted from him? And what's a girl to do?

Crushing Real Bad, 15

Dear Crushing:

When you put all your attentions on the guy you liked, he probably became intimidated and scared by so much focus on him. Now that you're into someone else, this guy can see you more clearly for who you are. It's human nature: when something is too easy and available, we tend to take it for granted. Now that you're no longer so available, your old crush is crushing back. What do you learn from this? Focus on yourself! You'll have a million guys after you then!!

Dr. Gilda

So, to attract the cool guys:

Gilda Gram   Be self-centered rather than boy-centered.

This approach to love works every time, but it's not a question of playing games. It's a matter of *loving* yourself and *being* yourself. Once you show a guy that you're the author of your life, he becomes more interested in seeing how he can be part of it. Then he suddenly begins to apply his hunter skills from his ancestors. He's ready to jump through hoops to try to get you to care.

Maybe at one time you thought of yourself as a geek, but now you're an It Girl goddess (or on your way to becoming one!), and you'll accept only the very best treatment from a man. This guy senses that, as an It Girl, you won't let your *he-meter* affect your *me-meter*. He knows that if it turns out that he's not a good guy, it will simply be good-bye. You have no patience for the guy who's adoring today, ignoring tomorrow. You want someone with two feet on the ground who calls when he says he will, and who keeps his word about everything he says. He knows you know you have choices, and that you'll ditch him if his behavior doesn't meet your needs.

It's your call to determine whether he's ready for commitment. Later, you'll see if he's long-term material. He knows that unlike other guy-crazy girls, you won't ever obsess over him because if you're gonna obsess over anything, it will be your own life. For you, love must be a give-and-take. He'll have to prove that he deserves you. He knows that you believe in yourself, and nothing he says or does will change that. If he doesn't support your greatness, he's outta there.

Dear Dr. Gilda:

I'm a 19-year-old sophomore in college. I love to travel and I have been to Europe four times, including studying abroad in the Czech Republic. Next semester I will be in Russia, and after that I'll study in Tahiti. My point in telling you this is that I am focused and I have an idea of what I want to do with my life. When I am at school, I want to travel, but when I come home, it is a little different. I still want to do a lot, but I also think about my future with a guy and kids.

My mom wants me to have kids now! She wants me to do what I want, but I think she'd prefer that I "settle down." During the summer, I met a guy from Portugal who was visiting his relatives here. He decided to move to the United States. Now that I am on school break, we have been seeing each other and it seems perfect. I don't want to "Bet on the Prince!", but I don't think any girl could ask for more. He is everything I would want in a guy for my future. He is family-oriented, he wants kids the same time I do (at about 27 years old), he is good-looking and has a good body, he likes everything about me, compliments me and thinks I am great, he pays for everything, likes to work, respects my needs and wants, and the list goes on.

So, what's the problem? He says he wants to be with me, but I am leaving and he said he is not going to "wait." He says he doesn't want a girlfriend, but if I were here, he would. He doesn't go out of his way to meet women, but if he does meet someone else, what will happen to us?

At this age, I feel that I shouldn't even be thinking about things like this, but you can see why I would want to keep him. I don't know if I should tell him how I feel or what. Should I let him know? He should be understanding because he wants to be with me, too. I think sometimes that he is sad that I am always leaving to go somewhere. He knows that I have a lot of goals, but those would come after I finish school. I don't know what to do. I could use advice from someone other than my mom or friend, and that's why I'm writing to you. Thank you and take care.
                                                              Meredith

Dear Meredith:

Wow! Your life sounds wonderfully fulfilling. But now you're torn between what your mom is pressuring you to do and what your heart is telling you. You sound amazingly excited about your life, and it would be ridiculous for you to give that up for a future with someone you know so little. You should know that there are some guys who are simply into the chase, and as soon as a woman gives up her entire life for them, they turn around and dump her. This may not be the case with your guy, but these things do happen, and you should be aware of them. In addition, when someone walks away from a fabulous career or opportunity for a love interest, often during the first argument they have, the resentment is thrown out to the other with,

"Look what I gave up for you." So never believe you must give something up for someone you supposedly love.

You must continue to do the things you are so excited about. In fact, when you do these things, it makes you a much more exciting girlfriend. While you're away, your guy ought to do the things that fill his heart also. Sure, it would be difficult for a while with you both missing each other, but that would not be forever, and each of you would have the wonderful opportunity of beefing up your skills to make yourselves even more marketable when you return to a life together—if that is going to happen.

Whatever you do, this is not the time for you to settle down and have babies, as your mom would like. At least you and your guy have already decided that that's not in your immediate future. Yes, he may be everything you THINK you want right now, but at the beginning, every love affair seems perfect. Without sounding trite, only time will tell. You are certainly not prepared to give up what you already have on your plate to spend your life without your college degree. You have such a wealth of opportunities that are not available to most people, it would be a shame to walk away from them. But this does not mean that you and your guy could not meet each other in different parts of the world while you're apart.

For the time being, enjoy every moment for what it

is with your boyfriend. By all means share your concerns with him. Let him also open his heart to you about his. When two people love each other, they want their partners to fulfill their dreams, as they fulfill their own. It makes for better and healthier romance.

Please let me know what you decide to do. But whatever happens with your guy, continue the life you love!

Dr. Gilda

Without knowing it, Meredith is an It Girl. She is focused on the things she loves, and is intent on fulfilling her goals. The only problem is that now she's torn. Her mom believes she should "settle down" and raise babies. (This may be her mother's value system, but it's apparently not Meredith's.) To add to that burden, her new guy is quietly pressuring her to abandon her dreams and set up new ones with him. Because she's being pushed to choose between her goals or a guy, she's in conflict. Remember, a guy in a girl's life should *enhance* what she's already got going for her, not try to prevent her from achieving it. Meredith needed to hear that from me. She also needed to hear that she could postpone an immediate relationship commitment until she was more ready.

Gilda Gram   If he's mine, I can't lose him. If he's not, I don't want him.

In other words, if this guy is meant to be with Meredith in the years to come, he'll be there. If he's wise, and he really thinks she's worth the wait, he'll spend his time making himself more desirable while she continues her school and travel. During her time at school, Meredith has been sharpening her scholastic skills along with her travel experiences. What she hasn't had is many interactions with the opposite sex and consequently hasn't become aware of the basics of relationships. Understanding guys and relationships is like studying an entirely different subject. Some people can be brilliant in school yet unsophisticated and immature in their interactions with men. From this experience, she can at least build her awareness of what it takes to be in a partnership.

This guy Meredith has met might be terrific, but he could also have some qualities that could disappoint her. A guy who would want his girl to give up the things she loves might really be envious of her success and achievements. He might also be jealous of all the positive attention she earns from her triumphs. In addition, he could simply be feeling left out of her life because she has so many other interests that don't necessarily include him. These might all be warning signs that an It Girl should recognize as soon as she can. But only time will tell, and if Meredith follows my advice, she'll take her time, wait and see, and reserve the right to decide later.

It Girl principles are principles that reflect a girl's inner strength. When a girl is strong inside, she attracts strong and sensational guys. Suddenly, *ta-da* . . . her biggest problem becomes which guy she should choose from all the cool guys who are interested in her. What fun *that* will be!

To reach Dr. Gilda Carle:

Web site: www.drgilda.com
E-mail: drgilda@drgilda.com